# SEE YOU
A Badass Guide to Getting
# RECLAIM YOU
Out of Your Own Head and
# BE YOU
Mastering Your Life

Donna Lavill

First published by Ultimate World Publishing 2023
Copyright © 2023 Donna Lavill

ISBN

Paperback: 978-1-922982-46-9
Ebook: 978-1-922982-47-6

Donna Lavill has asserted her rights under the Copyright, Designs and Patents Act 1988 to be identified as the author of this work. The information in this book is based on the author's experiences and opinions. The publisher specifically disclaims responsibility for any adverse consequences which may result from use of the information contained herein. Permission to use information has been sought by the author. Any breaches will be rectified in further editions of the book.

All rights reserved. No part of this publication may be reproduced, stored in or introduced into a retrieval system, or transmitted in any form, or by any means (electronic, mechanical, photocopying, recording or otherwise) without the prior written permission of the author. Any person who does any unauthorised act in relation to this publication may be liable to criminal prosecution and civil claims for damages. Enquiries should be made through the publisher.

**Cover design:** Ultimate World Publishing
**Layout and typesetting:** Ultimate World Publishing
**Illustrator:** Stephnie Robertson
**Editor:** Victoria Pickens

Ultimate World Publishing
Diamond Creek,
Victoria Australia 3089
www.writeabook.com.au

# Salute to the Author

"The information in this book are more than just words to Donna. Donna lives her life actively practicing the skills, knowledge, and tools that she has garnered over a lifetime of extremely challenging experiences. She is living her values, living her dream. May the reader benefit from that dream."

**Jo-Anne Hamilton**
B.A. (Psych); Grad. Dip. App. Psych; Dip. Clin. Hyp;
M. Couns; M. Human Factors Psychologist; Hypnotist;
Neuropsychotherapist

"Donna writes her truth, generously sharing her lived experience and life lessons to provide this self help guide. Readers will find it anything from life changing to the push they need to be their all. A great guide to help you on your way towards an ant free picnic of life!"

**Tina Hardin**
BSc BBus (MIS)

"Donna has shown us all, that insignificant interactions on the part of others can have momentous impact on individuals that can shape their lives interactions. We all can resonate with her story."

**Sonia Cattley**
PhD, M.Education

# I Give Thanks

To the reader, I wish you happiness, peace, strength, and serenity as you courageously climb the ladder of life one rung at a time.

To my community of friends, now and always for your love and support along my life journey.

To my family and friends watching over me from the next life, I feel your presence in my heart every moment.

To my life and book collaborators:

My therapists over the years, especially the brilliant Jo-Anne Hamilton who guided me gently as I reclaimed the me within.

My book illustrator, we finally collaborated on a project, a big thumbs up to my friend and talented artist Stephnie Robertson.

My techie housemate and friend Laura Lawrence who, on many occasions, prevented my computer from being thrown at the wall.

The Ultimate 48hr Author team of geniuses who worked hard in making my dream become a reality.

# Disclaimer

Within the book are many of my personal stories, while telling them I have stayed true to my memories of the events. My perspective may differ from others who were there at the time as these are my own personal tellings. I have deliberately left out many names of the innocent and guilty parties, apart from myself, of course, for moral and legal reasons.

While the advice and information in this book worked for me and is what I believe to be accurate, there is always risk involved and I, the author, along with the publisher specifically disclaims any liability, loss or damage caused or allegedly caused by this book and accept no responsibility for inaccuracies/omissions in this book. This includes any adverse effects or consequences resulting from suggestions, exercises, and advice in this book. This book is not a replacement for professional medical advice so please do not use this book if you are not willing to assume the risk.

Some material may be sensitive to the reader. These topics include bullying, sexual assault, substance overuse/abuse, suicide, death, and grieving.

This book may trigger painful memories and or reactions.

If the content is more than you can manage, please reach out to www.lifeline.com.au or your own local counselling service.

# Contents

| | |
|---|---|
| Salute to the Author | iii |
| I Give Thanks | v |
| Disclaimer | vii |
| Chapter 1: Understand It | 1 |
| Chapter 2: Conquer It | 11 |
| Chapter 3: Trust It | 25 |
| Chapter 4: Silence It | 39 |
| Chapter 5: Energise It | 51 |
| Chapter 6: Focus It | 63 |
| Chapter 7: Face It | 73 |
| Chapter 8: Share It | 85 |
| Chapter 9: Own It | 95 |
| Chapter 10: Know It | 107 |
| Chapter 11: Respect It | 119 |
| Chapter 12: Control It | 127 |
| Chapter 13: Go For It | 139 |
| About The Author | 149 |
| Free Downloadable Online Resources | 151 |
| Endnotes | 155 |

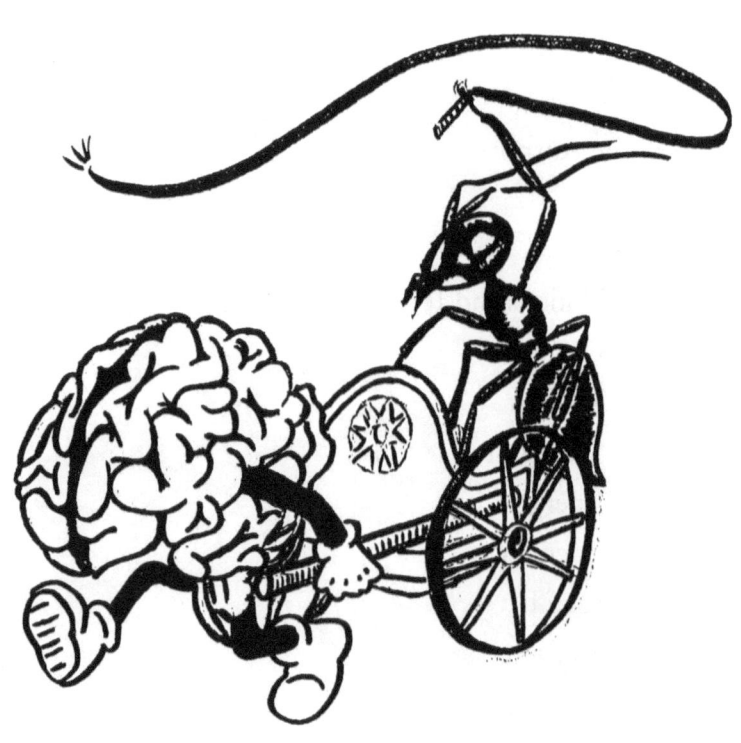

Chapter 1

# Understand It

Hello reader, how do you become a badass like me? This guide I'm writing for you is how I mastered my own life. How I got out of my own head, and how you can follow in my footsteps.

First up, automatic negative thoughts, or as I refer to them, ANTs. What are they and how do we get them? ANTs are habitual, non-conscious thoughts. Thoughts that come into your mind as you are going about your daily life. They affect your mood and your actions. For example, you might be walking along and thinking to yourself, '*Wow, that lady over there looks gorgeous in that dress.*' Then in jumps your ANTs with, '*I'm looking like a slob today.*' Or you see someone and think, '*That guy, he is always so popular, I'm just a loser.*'

Well, I see you. Yes, you, special human. You are wonderfully unique and perfect, just as you are. I learnt that as much as I am like others, I am also way different too. Different is good; it's interesting, regardless of what all the sheep say. Don't believe them, after all, it's you and your life, it's your values that make you beautiful and unique in the universe.

How do I tackle these ANTs? I know you want to know the secret to managing your negative thoughts; the techniques to stop bullying yourself from inside your own head. Well, let's get to it and begin finding the secret to your own success.

By now you have realised long-lasting success doesn't come overnight. It takes time. It takes courage. It takes effort. You need support from others in your life as well as from within yourself. Your ANTs get in the way of that. Also, if you're not living a healthy lifestyle, then how do you expect to be able to achieve success? It's okay to have the occasional little slip up here and there. That's human. That's normal and natural. Occasionally you might need a little bit more help. At times you may need to look for professionals or prescription medications to aid you in slowing your brain down, in calming you. That doesn't by any means make you a failure at all. It's just another little tool to help you along your journey.

By mastering your ANTs, you will become more self-aware, more self-curious, and you'll start living more in the moment. You will create a lifestyle that is loving. Surrounded with a community where you belong and can maintain your health, both inside and out. You'll take notice of what's around you, what's happening inside your body, and inside your own mind. ANTs start small, and throughout life you feed them, allowing them to grow until they're big and strong. By learning how to place the reins on them, finally seeing your ANTs for what they are, you can achieve so much more in your life. Study, challenge and starve them until they fade away. This will let you allow happiness to grow in the place where they were living. This is the only way you can truly become the you that you've always dreamed of.

## Understand It

How has life been working for you so far? I mean, there's this one quote that keeps coming back to me:

> *The definition of insanity is doing the same thing repeatedly and expecting a different result.*[1]

Is that what you've been doing?

I know it is what I did for a long time. Pesky ANTs cause you to repeat actions and are some of the main causes of ongoing low self-esteem and loneliness. Feeling like you are the only one in the world who experiences things the way you do or has the thoughts you have, like you are not worthy of succeeding in life and love.

ANTs can cause such anxiety and depression in our lives but there is a way to get over that. There is a way to achieve, to succeed, and be confident again. Just like when you were born. I'm sure you've noticed children are so free. They just run into the wilderness, into the unknown. They know to get out there and just be and do. They climb that jungle gym, run out into a field, and kick a ball without a thought. Even when they first learn to walk, somehow, they just know how to get up. They bend their knees and not their back. It's as we age that we pick up bad habits along the way. We forget to listen to our instincts. We lose faith and cease trusting ourselves. When ANTs get too loud, they become insurmountable and they build a wall in the way to stop you from achieving your goals, your dreams, even your daily routines.

## Story Time

From as early as I can remember, I formed ANTs that told me I was not worthy of love from anyone. As soon as I entered Kindergarten at school I was bullied by my fellow peers. To be completely honest, at times I may have even bullied them back in an inane attempt to regain control. All those years of being tormented, they stayed with me. Each experience imprinted on my brain. Long after my bullies were gone, my brain kept that imprint, and my own ANTs became my tormenters. Looking in the mirror all I could think was the words those bullies said to me all those years ago and it saddened me even more. Made me want to cover myself up. To somehow bleach my skin white, straighten and dye my hair blonde. Yes, my tan, my beautiful, dark curls that I now love are the same ones I once detested.

In early high school I told one of my classmates I wanted to be a model. She responded with, "Oh God, Donna, you can't possibly be a model. There aren't any black models in Australia." That was that. Dream squashed; ANTs created. Looking at myself today, I realise I'm not even black. I'm kind of brown and I'm proud of that. I think brown is beautiful. As an innocent child of around six, I didn't even really realise there was a difference between brown and white until it was pointed out to me. That was unfortunately the beginning of the racial divide in my own brain. My white adoptive parents had no idea how to combat this. The schoolgirl also told me I was not tall enough to be a model. Models, had to have slender bodies and long legs. I was barely five foot tall at the time. To her I wasn't the picture-perfect model that she'd seen in the magazines or on the television here in Australia in the seventies and eighties. In her mind, and then in my own, I could never be that picture of Australian cultural perfection.

What she didn't know was I didn't want to be a model to show off my beauty. I thought I was ordinary looking. I wanted to be a model because they got to wear the gorgeous fashionable clothes I couldn't afford. I wanted to learn how to do my makeup the way they did. To style my hair so beautifully like the models and actors in Europe and America did. I just thought it was such a creative career. I wanted to be a part of it. With her words, she had completely decimated my dream, my hope to become beautiful. My craving, my passion for talent and artistic creativity. I started relating my race, colour, and hair with the inability to be artistic. It's funny how the brain twists things around until one day you don't even remember when that opinion of yourself, that ANTs, first came into existence. Who knew it would

## Understand It

lead me to author this book to help in saving you and others from a life of disappointment and pain. To lead you towards a life of success in reaching for and achieving all your hopes and dreams.

When I was eleven, my parents enrolled me in the St. John's Ambulance Brigade Cadet Youth Program where I became a Cadet. Ordinarily at that time, Cadets had to be at least twelve to sit the first aid exam. My parents explained to the trainers I had been raised a year in school due to my academic achievements. They convinced the trainers that despite all my friends being a year older than me, I shouldn't be discouraged or rendered unable to take this big step with my peers. They allowed me to do the exam at eleven and I aced it. I got one hundred percent on the exam, the top of my class. It shocked my parents and peers, and it most definitely shocked me. I still have the trophy on my shelf. I had been bullied and told so many times by my peers I wasn't very smart, so getting one hundred percent on an exam while being a year younger than all of them, well, it left me stunned. I felt intense pride.

I continued with St. John's until I was sixteen, then applied for nursing at nineteen. This is where my journey of empathy truly began. I was around people of all ages, all races, and in their most vulnerable of their times. This was when I realised that so many people had negative thoughts about themselves. Thoughts that stopped them healing both physically and psychologically. One sentence I repeatedly heard from my patients was, "I just can't do it!" And I realized that I was saying those same words to myself all the time, stopping me from succeeding as much as it was stopping them from gaining their health back. It was time I found a way to understand those ANTs. To clear them and get my patient's and myself to move forward in life, believing instead that *'They can, I can!'* Day by day I began to tell them, *"Maybe just give it a try because I believe in you, I think you can."* I aided every single one of my patients with this mantra to get well.

I noticed that others I knew, had the same ANTs issues. My ex-partner had challenges because she left school before the end of Year 10. She had been told by so many people she was stupid, but I could see the smart in her. I knew she had a brain, and I knew that she could learn to use it more effectively. She had dreams of being a welder. Herein lay the problem; to get into a welding course, you had to have a passing grade at Year 10 level of high school. She of course, had not achieved that. Her dream was over, she was fatalistic. Just as my parents had done for me, I spoke to the trainers at the course. I said to them surely there was something she could do that would gain her entry into this welding course. I was determined to assist her in achieving her goal to be a welder.

The course administrator thought hard and came up with a way. As she was a mature age student, if she can sit a mathematics and an English test and pass over 60%, then she might be able to gain entry to the class. So, there we were in our thirties, her studying and me coaching her. I helped her to learn different formulas and I encouraged her to keep striving forward with her mathematics practice lessons. I had her read news articles and write out for me opinions about the things she'd read. I corrected and improved her writing skills with some spelling and grammar rules. Though, without her realising at the time, she did all the work.

At every turn she kept saying, "I can't do this, I don't know if I'll ever be able to pass."

I said to her at the time, "If you want it, I know you can do anything you put your mind to."

This is where the help of a person close to you in your life can really assist in quieting your ANTs. She went on pass the two tests with 90% and 100%. Later she enrolled in the welding course and became a welder, getting a job. She even started doing projects for herself and friends at home.

A group of friends and I were incredibly proud of her and her achievement. We got her a special present on her birthday, we put all our funds together and bought her a home mig welding machine.

She was elated. This was, I would say, one of the biggest educational achievements in her life. To be seen as someone with enough smarts to achieve this dream was insurmountable in increasing her self-worth and lowering her self-doubt. Self-doubt can be an immense issue in your life.

I helped her and I've helped many people. I can help you. I'll take you through breaking down your ANTs one by one in easy steps. One rung at a time to climb that ladder to success so you can beat your own ANTs too.

## Discovery Time

Why do we have ANTs? Well, something I didn't mention earlier is that ANTs are our own brains protection from danger. They only become a problem when they get out of control. No one wants ants ruining their perfect picnic. And we all know no matter how many times we brush them off they keep coming back to the food. Step back in the time, early cave dwellers would walk out of their cave, go off on a hunt. At times they would come across an animal that they knew they could not slay. If they encountered that animal and were injured, they would be less likely to go near that animal again. Were they to keep attacking, the animal would be most likely kill them. Similarly, if they encountered another cave dweller, or even another tribe, and there was an argument where maybe someone was maimed, hurt, or injured, then they would be less likely to try to encounter that same group again. ANTs warned them to be on their guard, to keep away or if they planned to confront either the animal or tribe, they would most definitely come with weapons.

Here in this book, I'm going to give you those weapons. They may not be tangible; they will often be gentle reminders that the danger is sometimes all too imagined. But what if occasionally the danger is real, you ask? It's okay, there is a way to discover which is which. You will work on that too. The physical responses you get when you react to ANTs can be terrifying and stop you in your tracks. ANTs can prevent you from moving forwards, backwards, even from moving at all. At other times, ANTs can cause you to run. You may feel tension, sometimes a tightening in the stomach, a jaw clench, a racing heartbeat. You could even get nausea and vomiting. Your vision can become blurry. There are so many physical responses you can have, and these are all controlled by your own brain chemistry. To put it simply is just the nuts and bolts of our emotion interacting with your physical body. Your nervous, muscular, cardiac, and pulmonary systems.

The hypothalamus, the pituitary, the adrenal gland. Really, these words all just are names of parts of our bodies that are used to create a homeostasis. To put it simply these are how our bodies create a way of maintaining balance. I may be a nurse, but I'm not going to go into depth with all these complex medical terms. That's not why you're reading my book. Our hormones do assist in controlling everything from appetite, sexual behaviour, and emotional responses to our temperature. Even our daily physiological cycles, for example, our sleep cycle. What helps you to battle and win over your ANTs, to find a balance in your psychological needs? How do you satisfy your physical needs? How do you find a sense of belonging, self-esteem, love in your life? How do you feel safe? That's what you will discover as you read on.

## Action Time

This is your first exercise assisting you in creating self-encouragement as you go through the book. You may have heard in passing of words of affirmation. Now, there are a myriad of ways people use affirmations. They can be complimentary words of kindness that come from others, but I suggest you start from within. Begin by giving yourself positive feedback to counter the ANTs. It just takes a little practice. Here's how you recognise and understand what your specific ANTs are. By identifying them it will make them easier to squash in the future.

- **Mirror Work**

Firstly, to start doing mirror work. It's time to grab a pen and get your Badass Diary going. I have provided a link at the end of the book free for you to download, so please print it and grab a pen. Next, all I need you to do is stand in front of the mirror, even if it's while you're brushing your teeth. Okay, when I say while you're brushing your teeth, I don't mean a five second fast scrub, I mean a full, steady, slow two-minute brush. Set a timer if you need to and just drift into your thoughts as you look in the mirror. What thoughts come to you when you're looking in the mirror? It is important that you allow yourself to think those thoughts very briefly and be curious about them. Do not give into the emotion of them. Just recognise the thoughts. Write them down in your notebook.

You'll work more on them later, but for now, just identify those thoughts. The biggest ANTs on those pages are the ones your mind, body and soul are screaming out for you to deal with. Carry the little notebook around with you and whenever any ANTs enter your mind, free yourself by jotting them down in the notebook for future reference.

Now importantly: to each ANT you say *'thank you'* to your brain for identifying it. You have probably had it for a long time so choose to write this ANT on the notebook page now. You will use the tools you are learning to deal with this and every ANT, one at a time.

## Reward Time

This is a journey. We've come to the end of the first chapter and already you're starting to learn a little bit about your ANTs. It's time to give yourself permission to do something nice for yourself. It can be something simple like a sweet treat, a walk, patting the dog, stroking the cat, or sitting outside and listening to the birds, whatever works for you. The main thing is that you have taken the first step and sought understanding by picking up this book and see how much you have learnt so far. Now be fearless and turn the page to start squashing your ANTs that you have just discovered.

# Chapter 2

# Conquer It

Now you've learnt what your ANTs are and while discovering them you may have experienced some apprehension. While it's all-consuming, fear is only just an unpleasant emotion caused by the threat of danger, pain, or harm. And notice I say threat. This is the definition of the word fear, and fear is not always a real tangible thing. It is not self-evident.

What is fear to you?
Does fear stop you from doing things or does it inspire you?
Or does fear to push you forward in your life?
What does fear do to your brain, your body?
What are your responses to fear?
How does fear create illnesses in your body?

Your ANTs are your fears; what you want the most or the least in life. Places you want to go, things you want to do. Your hopes and dreams. They can be the thought of not achieving them. Sometimes the thought of achieving them will bring your ANTs out to play. ANTs really do love a sugary treat, so wherever your sweet fear is, that's where they're going to congregate. Just remember as you are going through this book that you are totally worthy of taking time to work on yourself. Your time and effort facing these ANTs is not wasted. If you are going to beat the ANTs, you are going to need tools and preparation as:

*Prior preparation prevents poor performance*[2]

There are different variations on this. In Australia, we often say, "prior preparation prevents piss poor performance." However you choose to put it, there's so much you can gain as you plan to take back control from fear while making choices in your life. Have you ever found yourself getting defensive and overreacting to those perceived threats? This too can change. You can have pride in your achievements and reach for the things you've always wished to do. Have clarity in moving forward, beating procrastination where it stands. If you don't make these changes, you will continue to dawdle, to put off today until tomorrow and never achieve your dreams of success. Feeling the victim, like someone who just never could. Someone who thinks the world is against you. Oh, Chicken Little, the sky is not falling!

I talked a little about some ANTs that I and my previous partner had, but I want you to start exploring your own an and I want you to do ODC. That's right, not OCD (obsessive compulsive disorder). I want you to think of ODC; Origin, Discovery, and Creation.

Starting with your ORIGIN first. Your fears, where do they come from? They come from the past, but specifically where and when?

Next in DISCOVERY of your ANTs and uncovering the precise fears within them. So, what is it that you don't think you can get in life?

Thirdly CREATION of the life that you want, need, and deserve by crushing those ANT fears. When you identify the goals in your life, conquer your fear, you can set forward steps to achieving them.

## Story Time

- **Origin**

My biggest ANT was something my primary school teacher said to me over and over. I just couldn't understand as I got older why a primary school teacher would say such a thing to a child, to a student. She said, *"You are never going to succeed at anything unless you concentrate."* Of course, my brain stored this, but it missed the *"unless you concentrate"* part in my memory bank. Over the years I told myself, *'You are never going to succeed at anything.'* I realise now her intended meaning, *"If you concentrate you can succeed."* I wish she had said it like that. If you come at someone with negatives immediately off the bat, then they're only going to hear and store the negatives. They're going to switch off before the positive, which will just fly over their head. I allowed positives to fly high over my head many times in my life. Now I search for them instead of listening to the negatives. I went on for years not realising that I could succeed if I put my mind to it and concentrated.

A friend of mine said to me, "Donna, you've achieved so many things in life. What do you mean you're never going to succeed? You already have. You're a nurse, you've danced and acted on stage, you've even travelled abroad by yourself. I could never do those things." My quick retort was, "Oh yeah, but they're easy and you could do these things too, anyone could." Later, I thought about what I'd said, I was giving others the advice I should have been giving myself. *'You can and have done these things.'* That's when I thought back to the past and I recognised where that ANT had originated from, where it was born.

- **Discovery**

I realised one day I was afraid that if I did succeed, I wouldn't know what to do next. My life would become directionless, have no meaning. I don't think I was afraid of failing. I was more afraid of not knowing how to take pride in my own achievements. Not knowing what steps to take, which of my dreams to make come true next. Achieving goals and dreams leads to more steps and I wasn't ready to plan the next step. It all sounded like too much arduous work. I was frightened of what people would say, terrified others would be critical or jealous of my success. Maybe they would use me and my success for their own gain. What if friends just walked away from me because they couldn't handle my success. All these ANTs.

Turns out most people want to be around successful people. It helps them to strive for achievement themselves. Successful people foster success in others. The support and encouragement that we give to each other, helps each of us to rise above any fear that we may have had. There is something to be said for groups coming together and being stronger as community.

- **Creation**

I repeatedly informed my friends there was no way I could go back to university in my thirties. *'I wasn't smart enough to study at university level. I'd barely made it through my Year 12 high school studies'* and *'I had only done a nursing diploma through on-the-job training in a hospital'*. It was a shame you see; I had always dreamed of going back to university and studying drama.

I wanted to audition. I wanted to act. I wanted to learn everything about performing on the stage, on tv. I wanted to do it all. I still had that artistic little girl inside of me, but even so, I wasn't listening to my own advice. Luckily, I had good advice coming from my friends. Encouragement and help, remarkably like what I would later give to my own partner. At thirty-one I did it. After my friend's coaching and support I passed the mature age entrance exam. I went to university and at thirty-four I finished my Bachelor of Arts degree. I thought it would be lovely to do a stage show. I set out to look at auditioning for something. There were no roles out there at the time, no characters written for someone who looked like me, sounded like me. That's when another friend said, why don't you just write your own show?

*'No, I can't do that,'* my ANTs screamed. Later I pondered, maybe I could. I contemplated why I didn't think I could do it. I didn't have all the knowledge. I didn't have a theatre company for support. I didn't have enough money. How on earth would I put it all together in six months for the Adelaide Fringe Festival in my hometown in South Australia? Well, I bit the bullet with one week to write up an idea and get it off to the Fringe with my registration money to join in on this adventure. To my surprise, my friends turned to me and said, *"Anything you need, we will help"* and help they did. I got through it. I wrote my first fifty-five-minute length play about my adoption story and painful losses in my life. I decided to gather a group of friends together for a reading just to get opinions on how it was going. I was terrified, *'What if they don't like it?'* I did it anyway. They loved it. They came forward with positive comments on how to change certain areas of the play to make them more appealing for a wider audience.

Here I go, I've got a show. Then it hit me; the next steps, costumes, staging, lighting, sound, a venue, advertising, directing, and rehearsing my own show. I had only four months more to go. Weeks later I was struggling with a venue that had gone through a change of ownership and now I had extra costs. Chairs, bar staff and a hostile venue owner. I couldn't stop now though, I was committed. Now, years later, as I look back, all the trials and tribulations at the time seemed insurmountable. That journey I was making was one of the biggest achievements of my life to that date. I did it. I performed for two weeks in front of audiences of up to fifty people at a time in that dingy second-floor venue. I became vulnerable on stage with my own story and received warm applause from the audience.

I ticked something else off my bucket list and no one could take that away from me. I had to overcome so many ANT fears to get there. *'Was I good enough?' 'Would the show be good enough?' 'Would anyone want to hear what I had to say, what I had to show them about my life?'* I conquered all those ANT fears. This is how I did it. I used my variation on the management tool *SMART Goals*.

*SMART being an acronym for Specific, Measurable, Attainable, Realistic and Timely.*[3]

These were created for success in the business world, so I set about working out goals for my artsy self. As I did my dream became an unobstructed vision of future reality.

## W.H.A.T. Goals

- **W x 5**

The - what, who, why, where, when. I wanted to be able to write, fund and produce my own show. To perform it myself, direct it myself. I wanted to convey the struggles of my orphaned life. I needed others to know they could survive hardship too. I knew of a small venue to hire. I'd find volunteers for operating the tech, lights sound and ticketing at the door. All for a two-week run at the 2006 Adelaide Fringe Festival. This was something that would contribute to my future goals. I really wanted to become a performer. I wanted to be a writer, and I knew that doing this show would help to start me on my way to reaching my goal of becoming a published author one day, and look, here I am.

- **How**

How was I going to know when I had reached my goal. I needed a way to evaluate my achievement. Well, I suppose the only way to know if I had achieved the goal was to put the show on stage. To not be in debt at the end of the run. I wanted to be able to show it to a reasonable sized audience of up to fifty people a night, over a two-week run. So, when I had performed the show to a group of people and had that applause at the end, I'd know I had achieved my goal. It would be a bonus if I could get a reviewer to come too.

- **Access**

Did I have access to all the tools needed to make it happen? If not, what would I need? I would have enough finances if I did four to five ten-hour agency nursing shifts a week until the month before the show. Yep, I had the acting and writing skills to make this happen. I had studied them at university, and I'd been on stage and backstage for many amateur theatre productions for ten years. I had learnt skills in lighting, sound, props, costuming. However, I'd still have to read up and ask advice from others. I had only performed in shows that others had directed, others had authored the stories then. This time it was mine. I knew I could write; I'd written some poetry, and I knew I had a story. So, I knew my ability was there, I had the resources to make it all come about. Yeah, it was possible I had access to all the resources I needed.

- **Time**

I had a time frame, a completion date. I wanted to do it at the Adelaide Fringe in 2006. So, by paying my fees and setting my date, booking my venue, and so on, I knew when it was going to happen—in 6 months in March 2006. A deadline, not an open-ended goal, there was no excuse to not get things done, I had to make and follow a plan. I could sit and dream for years about getting a show on stage, or I could knuckle down and get it done, so now to work out if I had the time to do this. Easy, I knew I was able to work hard for an abbreviated time. I would be able to set aside time out of each day after work, before work, and on my days off to write the show, to make it all happen. I planned out a diary of tasks. This was something important to me.

Done. I had a W.H.A.T. goal. The planning was one big tick. I knew my deadlines. Then I put the planner page down, and two weeks later I panicked. I hadn't started doing anything. Procrastination had set in. I had to look for a new tool that would help me to get started. I would sit and look at the page every day to write this show. I just couldn't move the pen on the page. My ANT brain kept saying to me, *'There's so many stories to tell but no one really wants to hear mine. Who would want to know about me, my adoption story?'* Where do I start? Oh, procrastination-causing ANTs, how was I to overcome these?

## Mind Time Cheat

I discovered a mind time cheat technique that tricks your brain into thinking that you won't be doing something for very long. Then before you know it, you're doing it for hours.

- **10/20/30**

I put it into action like this. I said to myself, *'I'll just do this for ten minutes'* and I set a timer. I randomly wrote anything down on the page that might be related to the show that I wanted to do. It worked. I sat down and for ten minutes and I wrote every thought down. Wow, it was quite easy when I gave myself the freedom to just blurt it out. I re-read what I'd written, and I thought, *'hmm, maybe I can do this.'* Over the next few days, I sat down a few more ten-minute time blocks. Later in the day I thought I might do a little bit more, I sat down and set the timer for twenty minutes this time. I went over the timer because I still had more to write. The next day I thought, if I could do over twenty minutes yesterday, I might try for thirty today.

I sat down at the same time the next day, and it was becoming a bit of a habit, the same time each day at the same desk writing for twenty, then thirty minutes. Thirty minutes turned into forty, and forty turned into an hour. After that I just kept plugging away day after day taking short breaks every hour. Short snippets of time doing tiny amounts of work added up. Always remembering I had to make sure that I would take regular breaks and not fatigue my mind. The moment you fatigue your mind is the moment you start to lose the momentum, the concentration lapses begin, and the ANTs start to creep back in. The ANTs that say, '*Oh, I'm really not very good at this.*'

Sometimes on a day off from my nursing job I would get four or five hours of work done. Days when I was working at the hospital for hours on end, I would get home and I was exhausted. I would take a break, put my feet up, do something pleasurable for a little while, then I would set about my mind time cheat technique. And it worked. At the end of four weeks, I had a show written. I really liked this idea of tricking my mind into getting things done. Setting aside a small block of time each day with my timer set, putting my mind to achieving my goal, each day at the same time. If you have a randomly timed lifestyle or shift work schedule like I do now, you can schedule tasks around it. I put alarms in my phone. It's about planning to be ready. Having my desk, my space set up and ready to go, and there I go. It became easy.

## Discovery Time

Decision making and prioritising can be really difficult when you are trying to decide on specific goals and specific timeframes. But as the famous slogan for Nike says:

*Just do it* [4]

Things only happen if you just do them. I read books trying to break the procrastination bug. I learnt that it's how you respond to fear that creates the issue in your life. You can choose. Push through and use the fear to energise and empower you or continue to let it defeat you. Remember…

*Fear is not the problem?* [5]

Your response to fear is.

Now, here is something for your imagination. You're at the bottom of a mountain and you start climbing. It's hard, really hard. When you get to the top of that mountain you feel triumphant. But then you look down and you think, *'Oh my God, how am I going to get back down?'* *'What if I trip and fall?'* You can't live on the mountain. All you can do is lean forward and head down over the rocks, through the trees. The only way is through. When you get to the bottom, you look back up in amazement. Pondering how you made it to the top and if you will ever get there again.

You will!

Fear will always be there. Whether you are at the bottom of the mountain or at the top. Fear will be there when you're successful. It'll be there when you're not. The way to conquer fear is to use it to power yourself forward.

## Action Time

So now...
How do you conquer fear?
How do you get started?
How do you convince your body that it's okay to just go through the fear?

- **Breathing**

You've probably already heard this, but, breathe. You will calm your body. It's a great technique, but you must breathe deeply. Shallow breaths won't cut it, won't break through your anxiety. You will just hyperventilate and faint, and I've done that before myself. I have immense arachnophobia, and I remember one day being at a party at my own home and at the sight of a spider in the corner of the room I began to hyperventilate. The spider moved and I ran from the room, tripped and fell, landing on the front lawn, unconscious. It's okay to laugh reader, I laugh at myself now, too.

But you don't want to be like the old me. You want to breathe.
Your aim is to breathe deeply and slowly.
To stop moving.
To look forward or close your eyes, whichever is most comfortable for you.
Take a long, deep breath in through your nose, opening your chest, allowing it to expand.
Feel your diaphragm, that lower muscle below the lungs, push down into your abdomen.
Allow your stomach to move outwards.
Don't hold anything in.
Relax, drop your shoulders.
Hold that breath for 1, 2, 3, even 4 seconds if you can.
Then open your mouth and very slowly let that breath out to the count 10.
Then open your eyes or adjust your gaze until you feel settled.
Strive forward up or down your mountain.

That's how you breath the calm in deeply. Keep going. One breath after the other and then another. Until you feel calm again.

- **Affirmations**

It's Badass Diary time again, open to the affirmations page.
When you were young, do you remember anything that was said to you that made you feel special?
That made you feel good, really good. Allowed you feel like you could achieve anything in the world. I want you to write it down now. Not to worry if you don't have any of your own now, I have plenty of affirmation creating ideas for you. For example, when I was young, my parents would always say to me, "Come on girl, you got this. You can do this." They would say that I was "the most beautiful baby on

the shelf at the adoption agency" and I believed them. I believed I was chosen because as they said, "I was special." Whenever I need to feel fierce, I just remember those words my parents said.

Remember your ANTs, your specific fears. It's time to set your affirmations around battling those. If you are wanting to get a new job, make more money, look more attractive, or even achieve a goal like putting a play on stage. Create positive words to say to yourself around those. For example, when I wanted to put this show on at the Fringe Festival, I would say to myself, "My writing will convey positive messages to people who need to hear them" and "I am a great actor." When I was fearful of how people would see me on stage, I would say to myself, "I am beautiful inside and out, people will see me for the wonderful talented woman I am."

I didn't believe it at first, but the more I said these to myself, the more I flourished, the more positive my thoughts got. The negative ANTs just seemed to wander aimlessly into the distance. It took time and practice, but with repetition, anything can be relearned. Persistence is an amazing skill.

- **Dreams Imagined**

It's time for you to imagine your dreams coming true. I want you to visualise them. I want you to see them, truly see them. Close your eyes and see them as if they are a moving picture that has already happened. Don't just imagine it, feel it. Feel the joy, the satisfaction as you are seeing that moving picture of your success going past your eyes.

How does the sensation of happiness make you feel?

Smile as you feel the warmth, the calming heartbeat, or the excited racing one. Take a breath; yes, you have now begun to believe you can accomplish something with your affirmations. You are not just imaging what you can do, you are feeling it.

## Conquer It

- **Letters and Diary Plans**

Time to move from thinking and feeling it, to writing it. It's time to make an action plan, get your Badass Diary open to write a short letter to your youngest self.
What would you tell yourself to do if you knew you couldn't fail?
If you knew there was no way you would not achieve this dream or goal. Believing anything is possible, what would you tell yourself?

Write that down.

That is your dream.

That's also where your ANTs live, next to where your fear is sitting, trying to tell you that you can't. But you've just written a letter to your younger self. Tricking the ANTs in your brain into seeing the possibilities.

Breathe. Take your time, but not too much, ha, ha, ha. Set affirmations for this dream. Imagine the dream coming true and plan it. Set those W.H.A.T. goals. Plan to start small and build using the 10/20/30 mind time cheat technique. Plan it all out in that Badass Diary.

## Reward Time

It is that time again. Give yourself a bag full of kindness, some relaxing rewards. Permission to get out there and daydream, let your imagination see puppies in the clouds, fish in the river, whatever tickles your fancy. Today, at the end of this chapter, it's time to take a walk. Smell the roses, as they say.

Now get to it. What fear will you choose to conquer first? Trust me, I know you can do it.

Chapter 3

# Trust It

I have questions for you reader.
Do you kick yourself endlessly for every mistake you make?
Do you ever forgive yourself?
Does unforgiving, relentless anger, frustration and hurt feelings hold you back from moving on and up?
Do you trust yourself, your instincts, your decisions?
When did you stop trusting yourself?
When did you stop trusting others?

There are so many important things you are going to learn about your trust issues and the art of letting go of your anger and pain, freeing yourself from your resentment of others. You will even break the emotional memories linking you to those who hurt you in the past. People who used, abused, or pushed you around. We've all got them.

Those who created the ANTs in your brain screaming that you are not good enough just because someone said so. Uncover how you can beat them into submission. You are also going to discover that emotional space to thrive, growing in your own self-confidence. To do this you must let go of anger and frustration, you must find forgiveness for others, and more importantly, you must find forgiveness from within for yourself. It is only then you can learn to trust your own choices, your own decisions, and go forward with your dreams and goals, those you rediscovered in Chapter 2.

It is entirely possible you may be having trouble getting those dreams and goals from Chapter 2 to become your reality. The reason stems from your ability to trust yourself in making your own decisions. If you don't get rid of this pain, anger, and resentment of yourself and others, it will eat away at you causing physical illnesses. High blood pressure (hypertension), and depression being some of the most common. All that mental anguish that's rolling around inside your own brain affects you physically too, not just mentally. This is widely recognised through the medical community. I'm sure you don't want to be known as the person with behaviours such as passive aggressive, hostile, or cynicism. No one wants to be described as a 'Negative Nancy' or difficult to be around. It is horrible to feel defensive, angry, anxious, and frustrated all the time. No one is born to that negative way of being, you learnt it. And what you have learnt, you can unlearn.

Of course, after you've behaved in those ways you end up knocking yourself and there begins the cycle. Where you behave badly, you regret it and then you react, inadvertently behaving badly again. Your self-esteem remains way down in your boots. These are the costs to you of not changing, of not following the steps outlined here in this chapter. Of not trusting that you can get past all these feelings, these emotions. You won't be able to move forward with achieving your passions, dreams, and goals unless you learn to trust your choices and decisions that will get you there to success.

# Story Time

It took me a long time to learn how to forgive myself. My ANTs yelled at me whenever I made a mistake. *'What I did was so unforgivable, I'm a terrible person.'* I realise now what I did was keep believing in those ANTs. Believing that others saw me as unforgivable, how could I forgive myself. When did this start? How did this happen?

When I was little, I stole a 50-cent coin from atop of my mum's desk. I went to buy lollies at the shop. I told myself I was borrowing it. When I got home, my mum tapped the desk and said to me, "Where has the 50-cent coin gone?"

Sheepishly I replied, "I don't know."

She looked me in the eye, and I looked away, and in that second, I knew she knew. She saw that I had lied. I could still taste those lollies in my mouth, but I felt terrible on the inside. I had the biggest stomach-ache that night, the lollies soured in my stomach with my guilt.

My mum said to me, *"You are a naughty, nasty child. How dare you steal from the hand that feeds you?"* She made me pay for the theft the next week when I had to do extra chores. She made go around and pick up all the dog poo in the garden, wash the dishes every night, clean the bathroom, and vacuum the house. Somehow this was to be my penance to wash my guilt away all for just 50-cents. That whole week, she looked at me with that mother's eye of *'You horrible child.'*

I just couldn't bear that she also saw me as horrible. She was just teaching me a lesson; I see that now. But at the time, my thinking morphed into the feeling that *'Mum hates me.'* Those sweet lollies also embittered in my brain. I said to myself, *'I'm a terrible person.'* I questioned why I did it. I believed she was never going to forgive me so how could I forgive myself for stealing that 50-cents? I felt like I was the worst person on earth at the time. Fast forward to years later and each time I borrow something from someone, if I am late or forget to give it back, I get that same feeling as if I've stolen it from them. As if I'm the worst person on Earth. I don't know how my brain took the 50-cent story and morphed it into ANTs that survived over forty years. I had to be rid of these ANTs that said, *'I always do unforgivable things, I am unforgivable, I'm a terrible person.'*

I held my 39th birthday party at my house. Displayed on the sideboard counter I had these cute little elephants that I had inherited after the death of my mother six years prior. They were just little ornaments, but she'd brought them when emigrating from the United Kingdom when I was just a baby. There were four of them. Always facing away from the door to, "Keep wealth and luck coming in," she said, and now they were mine. There were drunken shenanigans at the party. A few people had an argument, someone fell over. I don't really remember all the details now, but what I do remember was that when I got up in the morning to clean up, there were only three elephants on the counter. Not four, I recounted, only three. I searched on the floor, under all the chairs, the table. I moved furniture trying to find this fourth elephant. I could not find it anywhere, and I was inconsolable because just as I had witnessed my mother doing often, I had continued her habit over the years since her death of stroking each of the four elephants for luck as I passed by them. I felt my luck diminished by one.

Inside I knew someone, a friend, took it. I even looked in the bin to see if someone had broken it, thrown it away. It was nowhere to be found. I messaged everyone and asked them if they could just return the elephant. I was a woman enraged and obsessed. I didn't need to know who took it, I just wanted it brought back. I gave the option to just drop it off anonymously in my letter box. Yet I still did not receive the elephant back, even to this day. For years after that party when I had people in my house, I scanned everywhere they went, everything they did. I could not forgive the person who stole the elephant. I was on guard from that moment onwards, unable to get past the fear that someone would steal something else. I couldn't settle the anger, hurt feelings that someone would come into my house and take something that had such sentimental value to me. I was left with a sense that I must have *'poor judgment skills'* as to who I let into my life and my home. I didn't know who to trust anymore. So, my ANTs said, 'trust no one.'

When I uncovered this ANT, I was enraged. Things that happened affected me in deeper ways than I could have ever imagined. The ANTs grew and grew until I would look at everyone sideways, untrusting. I didn't realise I watched them nervously, anxious that something would go missing, get broken. Subconsciously thinking that someone would betray my trust or behave badly towards me. I was defensive, angry, even hostile at times. These behaviours carried over into my work life, my friendships.

My ANTs of not being able to trust others and not being able to trust myself, brought forth feelings of anger and frustration. Now that I knew where my ANTs came from, I had to find a way to get past them. These ANTs had been festering inside my brain for too long. I needed a way to learn to forgive others and myself. So, I sought that out, found and adapted some amazing apology and forgiveness concepts I so deeply needed. Some of those are the five languages of apology, expressing regret, accepting responsibility, making restitution genuinely repenting and requesting forgiveness[6]

I realised that we have all learnt to apologise and forgive in diverse ways. Some just simply say *sorry* and then move on, others need only to see a change of behaviour to recognise the person is repentant. Then there are those who need the conversation, an explanation and change of future behaviour along with the apology. I realised I needed them all. This is not just how I want others to apologise to me but also how I apologise to others. I do not forget but I do forgive. I wanted the elephant thief to return the elephant, apologise, and accept responsibility with no excuses for their behaviour. I also wanted them to promise not to steal from me again, and I needed them to prove to me with future behaviour that they had changed their thieving ways. Only then, through time, could I forgive. I never got this from the elephant thief so how would I recover? How could I forgive and move on? I journaled and it worked. I never got the elephant back, but I let go of the anger at the thief.

To this day when I practice my apology/forgiveness tools, I feel freer, more positive, and less anxious. I don't hold onto anger and tension in my body anymore. Instead of being up around my ears, my shoulders now drop naturally. The tension causing headaches, neck pain, back pain and stomach aches that would leave me unable to work for days on end, dissipated easily and became a thing of the past. Along the way I discovered something that shocked me; as I sat down to write out how to forgive other people, it was easy to work my way through that. But to accept forgiving myself was another matter. I realised I wasn't only angry at the person that didn't return the elephant. I was also angry at myself for leaving the elephants out on display where they could be stolen. Forgiving myself was just way more important than forgiving the person that took the elephant.

On occasion I'd ask someone I felt I had wronged to forgive me. If they didn't grant that request, my frustration intensified. I hadn't been able to truly repent and apologise in my own way to them and have my apology accepted. *'Who do they think they are to not accept my apology?'* I guessed that this is the same thing that I've been doing to myself. I'd be saying to myself, *'It's okay that you did a bad thing, forgive yourself.'* But my ANTs were kicking back and saying, *'Hell no. You don't get to apologise to me. You don't get to fix this. You must live with this forever.'* It's kind of rude if you think about it. I wouldn't be happy with that lack of forgiveness from another person. Why on earth was I accepting that from my own brain?

So, yes, forgiveness truly does come from within. Fighting your ANTs even when they say, *'You are unforgivable'* turn it around and say, *'I can be forgiven, I forgive myself for all of the things that I have done wrong because I know I can make changes and not repeat those mistakes again.'* I did not want to live my life in a perpetual state of regret. I chose to find ways to accept responsibility, make apologies to my myself, change my behaviour, then truly forgive myself and move on.

I made steps forward in life without deliberating about every wrong step I had made before. I became able to trust myself again, starting with me, myself, and I. Only then moving on afterwards to forgiving others. I'll give you some practical tools in Action Time on how to follow this through.

Learning to trust myself and to trust others seemed near impossible. Somehow the bond between me and trust was broken. It wasn't really that I could see the break either. It was the ANTs inside telling me, *'No, they're lying. You know they're lying. They've done it before.' 'You have made this mistake before. You can't possibly think you could make a decision that would not lead to the same mistake.'* My ANTs had gotten so loud that every broken trust was like a cotton thread and my ANTs gathered them all to twist them into a strong rope. I was clinging to that rope. While dipping into my forgiveness toolbox of skills, questions came leaping out. Okay, so you've forgiven these people. You want to trust them, but who can you trust? You haven't made great decisions trusting in the past, so how can you make great decisions now? I needed to cut that rope, burn it, rid myself of those trust-fear ANTs.

I had unconsciously practiced not to trust myself or my own decisions so much that I was now stuck in quicksand, unable to escape and unsure who to throw a line to so as to save myself. Even though I had started to truly heal, I was still struggling to reach out and connect. Was it fear again, rearing its ugly head, or was it something new? I threw caution to the wind, and I pushed myself into friendships with people. Many that I should have been able to clearly see were totally unsuitable, untrustworthy. But I decided to look at everyone as being trustworthy until they proved me wrong. You can just imagine how that turned out. I went on date after date and I thought, *'wow, this person is great they could be the one to love me and help me love myself.'* Time after time I'd get drunk and make mistakes. Or occasionally they'd break my trust, like spiking my drink. I'd wake up the next morning unaware of where I was or who was laying in the bed next to me.

They are my stories, some funny and some tragic, for a future book. I'm not saying don't trust anyone, but life would be pretty boring if we didn't trust some people. So how do you decide which ones to trust and which ones not to trust? Then it's important to know who to trust with your personal, sensitive information too. You wouldn't go to work and talk about your sex life, and you wouldn't go to bed and talk about your confidential work contracts. Definitely a clever idea to set boundaries.

## Discovery Time

Trust differs in every single circle you move in. We will look at how you can create those trust circles at the end of this chapter as well.

It is obvious that not everyone's going to know everything about you. You are allowed to keep things to yourself, present yourself how you wish to be seen. In turn you are not going to know everything about them. Also, there are going to be some blind spots, things that people know about you that you don't realise about yourself and vice versa. No one knows everything, so sometimes neither of you have knowledge of some things. The best part, though, is a little mystery is a good thing, it keeps you curious and interested in developing more connection with others. The bits that you share together, the things that you both know about each other are the special moments. Think about the people in your life and where they fit in. Use this image to discover your relationships with others. It will help you to decide who to trust, communicate and share your life with.

You gain valuable perspectives learning from your past successes and your very human mistakes. Remember to look at them as a learning tool rather than a blaming tool so your ANTs will have nothing to feed on. When your ANTs say to you, *'You are so stupid for trusting that person,'* or, *'You shouldn't have done that.'* That's when you stop, look those ANTs square in the eyes and respond, *'Thanks for letting me know, but I choose to see this as a learning experience.'* Know that you

## Trust It

may have trusted that person but now know you shouldn't trust them again while knowing that there are other people you can trust. You will learn to look for the signs that someone is or is not trustworthy, their body language, the way they behave.

How perceptive are you?
Do you notice when people are unable to look you in the eye especially when you're trusting them with something important?
Do you realise when people are unable to share with you as you share with them your secrets?
Is there a lack of openness with the people in your life, from them or from you?
I want you to get curious as to why that may be.
Can you trust someone if you hear them gossiping about others?
Aren't you curious about whether they gossip about you when you are not around?
So don't give them so much information. Share your information with someone else who you have come to realise you can trust. Start with a small circle of people and work your way out.

## Action Time

- **Forgiveness Journaling**

Let's start with forgiveness. Healing one thing at a time. It's going to take a little while, but I'm sure you realise by now it is totally going to be worth it. Start with something small. For example, I forgive myself for getting drunk and compromising my safety, I know I can behave safer in the future. Start with something about yourself. And I want you to write this out. The structure goes as follows, and you fill in the blanks.

**I forgive** (who) **for** (what)

You will write this out seventy-two times for thirty-six days. Yes, that's right. It is a commitment. You need to repeat the same sentence over and over. If you miss a day, you start again. There's a trigger in the brain that when you do something many times it, the brain believes it. You will be surprised, like any practice, this does become easier with time. So even with the things you find most difficult to forgive, you can find a way to do it with this tool.

Get in the groove choose a thing first. Done the small one? Now move to the bigger things in your life, the things that are really getting in your way, the ANTs that shout the loudest at you.
Go on, get to it in your Badass Diary.
What will you choose to forgive yourself for first?
And then who else will you choose to forgive next?

- **Trusty Eggs**

Now, for trust, let's get creative in your diary. You want to build central circles of influential people in your life, those that you trust. You will be thinking about what you trust them with, when and how you share that trust. Some circles intersect and others are entirely separate, never meeting one another. Time to get creative. Make it as artistic as you want or do like I do, draw stick figure drawings, and write names.

Draw an egg. Put yourself in the middle of the yolk. Draw a little you or just write your name. Remember you can do this for as many circles of friends you have. You may be at the centre of more than one egg. Name each egg, what circle of people that is, i.e., family, work colleagues, book club, footy club.

### The yolk
The first primary circle is small and contains people with whom you have mutual trust. Place the drawings or names of the people that you can trust with most anything. Your romantic partner, or your closest friend whom you have known for a long time. People who have earned your trust in the past. People you can be vulnerable with.

**The white**
Your friendly acquaintances are here. Place here people that you share parts of, but not all, the vulnerable areas of your life with. People who are fun to be around. Preferably make them the positive people.

**Outside the shell**
Those you don't trust go here on the outer of your trust egg, no need to crack the shell for them. Place their names outside. Sometimes these are people who you may find unable to remove from your life or the negative people. You simply have little or no reason or need to trust them.

Now in each area of your egg list the things that you have, could, would share with them. For example: your home life, hobbies, joyous moments like weddings and births or sad ones like a family death.

Think about how or when you would share them; in person, or online. Would you tell them things on a work break time? You might confide a little more over the telephone. So that would be your how and when.

You don't have to complete this entire basket of eggy circles now, and they may change as relationships naturally do. You can add names to them, you can just leave them as nameless groups to add to later. Over time you will start to build more circles of trusted people within your life. Observe, see other friendships, watch their behaviours, and just learn by experience. No need to let the gates fly open, presenting too much of yourself to start with. But when someone you know proves themselves to be a trustworthy person, you can add their name. This is how we learn. We share in loving circles, we grow as a community. Don't go out and try and share it all at once. It's not necessary.

Now you've got structure, your people you can trust. You've got your gooey eggy circles. You can start to confide in your inner yolk people about your journey with this book. They may have already noticed changes in you as you travel to wellness and happiness.

## Trust It

So, are you ready to start forgiving yourself and forgiving others?
Who will you forgive first?
Are you ready to start sharing?
Are you ready to start trusting?
Who are you going to trust first?

I know you've got it in you.

## Reward Time

It's again time to break out and do something for yourself. Have a catch up with a friend, go for a walk, sit and have a coffee or tea, talk about life. Talk about this journey with someone that you have built trust with over time. There's no race here. No more thinking to be done. It's time to soar through your life. Speak now, organize now. Act now, right now. Trust yourself. I know you can do it.

Still more awesomeness to learn, see you in Chapter 4.

# Chapter 4

# Silence It

Are you a social butterfly or a Chatty Cathy? Sorry to all of you named Cathy.
Do others call you an attention-seeking blabbermouth?
Do you have times when you chat about inappropriate topics - at inappropriate times in inappropriate places to inappropriate people that you don't even know?
Do you later regret it?
Those times when you just can't seem to shut up. Are you often saying about yourself, I've got foot in mouth disease and I'm constantly changing feet.
Are you forever putting out your own fires?

Well, let me tell you, this is just another reaction to the ANTs telling you you're not feeling safe, you're not feeling comfortable. You're oversharing and it's so easy to do. We're all guilty of it sometimes, but for some of us who have high anxiety, we do it a lot.

There's a way to feel more secure and safe in places where you previously couldn't understand how to get around those uncomfortable silences in conversations. And there's methods to lowering the anxiety you have when you're in a social setting. It is something you can gain control over. If your ANTs are anything like mine, they'll be telling you *'When there's a silence, you must fill it.'* My talky ANTs tell me when there's a gap in the conversation it's because *'I am not interesting'* and *'The other person is going to turn and walk away and leave me all alone standing there by myself in that silence.'* We've all had those awkward moments where everyone just stares at each other and waits for the extrovert in the group to start talking again. Hoping they can talk just to fill the space, the void left behind with the absence of sound. You speak, trying to make it so there's no more discomfort but end up making yourself a vulnerable target. You can learn not to run your mouth off, not to overshare by telling everyone everything in one breath. It is possible to train yourself to keep things to yourself and only say them at appropriate times. To be honest, when you do overshare, you create more talky ANTs. Everyone wants fewer regrets over their own mouthy behaviour.

You can also learn how to listen more. Listening is one of those skills that is a bit of a lost talent these days. People tend to talk over each other. Learning to listen will help you to create the feeling of true connection to others. You'll build stronger bonds with others when you can listen to them. When you leave space for them to be able to talk to you as much as you talking to them. When you don't listen to people, you don't really get to know them or remember anything about them. Often the next time you meet them you will struggle to even remember their name. People will lose trust in you and won't bother to converse with you, because why share anything about themselves when you have shown that you don't care about them. You don't want to know. They don't matter. People will eventually avoid being around you and connections will be lost. At first meeting they feel like they're connecting with you. But later they only remember your name because you did nothing but talk and talk. You were interesting at first, but you just wouldn't shut up. You can't put your finger on why you end up feeling uncomfortable around others. You are also repeating the same things all the time just to fill gaps in conversation. Well, that is the cost of not changing.

## Story Time

Others always felt they knew me incredibly well. Really, they knew the same few things about me, things that I shared over and over. They didn't really know much about the real me. I felt disconnected. I was popular at parties but still felt alone in a room full of people. If only I'd known sooner that this uncomfortable, lonely way that I was living, could be changed. Trying to feel comfortable by incessantly talking ultimately led me into a place of confusion and self-harm. I had to start dealing with my talky ANTs. After raving on and on, switching from one topic to another for hours on end, people would say, "Oh my god, get your shit together, Donna." My over talking stemmed from my sense of loneliness growing up as an only child.

My parents would throw me in front of the family members or friends and get me to entertain them while they went off to make a cup of tea. So, I learnt to be the little entertainer. Everyone loved it and it was amazing being the centre of attention in a room full of adults all wanting to listen to me. I'd tell them about my day at school or how I'd been having fun playing with the dogs in the garden. But then there were times when it was just me and the dogs or I was all alone; I was bored and lonely. I'd have conversations with the dogs. If they didn't stay put, I'd time how long I could talk to a blade of grass or a flower. I'd talk about anything to everything. So, whenever I saw people, I was excited to talk to them and I just couldn't stop. It flowed over into school. I'd be sitting in class and wouldn't be able to stop talking to the kids sitting next to me, behind me or in front of me. Even sometimes to the teacher who would say, *"Donna, you need to stop. You talk too much."* And I'd say, *"Yes, but I just have this one thing to say, this one question."*

Strict, impatient teachers would throw me out of class to think about my behaviour. The understanding, kind teachers would say, "Yes, you always have something interesting to say, but now is not the time." I developed little ANTs in my head that whispered, *'you talk too much. Why can't you just shut up, Donna?'* So, on one hand, I really hated the fact that I couldn't stop talking, distracting others. On the other hand, I was proud of the fact that I could socialise easily, entertain people, and keep a conversation going no matter what. Even my father would often say, "oh, girl, you can talk the hind legs off a donkey and then teach it to walk again," and I thought that was great.

When I was being bullied at school, I would talk to the other kids from that bully's group. The kids who had bullied me the previous day were now being told by their own friends to leave me alone. They would say to my bully, *"Nah she's cool, you just got to get to know her."* All because somehow, I'd found a way to connect with others in the group. Though I hadn't really connected, I had just entertained them. My anxiety, my nervous chatter, trying to regain my composure, distracting myself and them was just a way to mask my fear. To hide the tension of being in their presence. I was just trying to be tough. It was my only way of coping with all the drama, all the conflict that was going on in the schoolyard. It worked most of the time, until I got to class, and the teacher made me stop.

Then I was banished from the classroom, left sitting in the corridor alone with the thoughts in my head while I was trying to learn the lesson of silence. While in class my brain wouldn't be quiet to let me concentrate and listen to the teacher. I just wanted to talk and not listen. Then before I knew it, I hadn't heard any of the lesson, instead I had been chatting to the kids next to me or in the corridor. Somehow, I couldn't slow my brain down because I'd gotten into a habit of always creating things to say and having no composure, no self-control to stop and put those thoughts away until later. Those thoughts were not always important. They didn't always need to come out of my mouth.

Later in life oversharing became quite a habit for me. There were times when I shared things that were totally inappropriate in places, like where I worked. I'd be there, we'd be operating on a patient, and I'd be talking about the guy I picked up on the weekend or the girl I broke up with last week, even the night I got drunk and fell over a tree trunk in the park—and it was inappropriate talk in my workplace. They'd all look at me and smile and laugh because maybe some of them had been through similar experiences themselves. But when they didn't share back, that's when it suddenly dawned on me, I was oversharing again, and it was the wrong space. I wondered why I did this, and the only answer was that people were trying to concentrate on their job, and I thought it was an uncomfortable silence. I really needed to learn to let them concentrate, let them do what they were doing, and just be in that silence, in that concentration space with them. Unfortunately, though, as I would start to realise this my nervous chatter would continue again, trying to regain my composure and distract myself from the shame that I was feeling over having overshared and I would then overshare more.

It became an endless cycle of one overshare after another. I often felt intelligent because I learnt something and just wanted to share it. But knowing stuff and being right is not always what's important. I would fight with my own two opposing beliefs at all costs, to whatever end. As onlookers listened on, I talked myself in circles, seemingly changing my opinion several times until I'd settle on a winning one. Only then was I satisfied, even though the argument wasn't with them it was me battling my own internal cognitive dissonance. Even if my views were unwarranted or unwelcome advice given to others, I still felt important and clever. It wasn't the best way to try to be liked, popular or interesting. It didn't make me cool. I even occasionally got into the habit of following others' lead and gossiping. Gossiping is such harmful chatter, and even though I had always prided myself on my kindness to others I ended up doing what I hated the most.

Back in 2015, I went to an art exhibition installation by Honi Ryan, Strange Embrace - mindful encounters social performance[7]. It was an amazing challenge for me and a huge bonding experience with a good friend of mine. She and I sat in the cultural centre art space in the Blue Mountains, New South Wales (NSW). We sat silently opposite each other taking turns to listen to each other's heartbeats with a stethoscope for 5 minutes. Then we each took a glass, we passed water from one glass to the other, over, and over, for 5 minutes again in silence. At first it was uncomfortable but then it became relaxing, we were connecting. Wow, in silence.

Later I experienced a similar bonding exercise with another friend, where we sat looking at each other silently. Looking into each other's eyes, just gazing, not in a loving way, just looking at each other. Not thinking of anything to say, not wanting to break that moment. It was uncomfortable just silently staring, not looking away. Just sitting, staring into her eyes for one minute in this beautiful space. I think it was more uncomfortable for me because I was the incessant talker of the two of us. I struggled. After the timer went off one of us was permitted to speak very briefly. Then the time went back on again and we had to sit and stare for one more minute. We took turns to speak but when I got to speak, I couldn't think of anything to say. Normally I had a hundred things I wanted to say. Now I just said that she had pretty hair. We went silent for one more minute, and she got to speak again. She thought I had pretty hair too. When it got down to the basics after that uncomfortable moment, we both had a compliment for each other, something positive. This is a wonderful way to be.

## Discovery Time

Our bodies do seem to sabotage us sometimes. We have stress hormones, cortisol and adrenaline from the adrenal gland circulating around in our bodies. They can give us a boost of energy telling us to fight or telling us to run, flight. Sometimes even telling us to fawn and fake our way through perceived danger. All in hope that just maybe the fear will subside, the threat will dissipate. It's always about threat. The threat of not being liked, of being alone, of looking stupid. Sometimes, the ANTs keep telling you to *'Keep your mouth going'* to try to fight, fawn or fake it through. But there is a way to regain your feeling of safety and quit that endless chatter for good. It's all about impulse control versus the gratification of your ego. Now, I like to think I'm not a very egotistical person, but we all have ego. We all like to receive attention, respect, and we all have a selfishness to us. Questioning in these moments what takes over: the impulse control, or the gratification of that ego, is the start of behavioural change.

It's about stopping and recognising when you're feeling those sensations of uncomfortableness in your body. Sensations that are telling you to run your mouth off because you don't feel safe in a quiet space. And remember, it's rude to talk over other people. It's inappropriate to finish their sentences as if they don't have an opinion of their own that you haven't already heard before. You don't already know what they're going to say all the time. You are really commandeering the conversation, and that's not fair on them. You are going to learn some new conversational listening skills and create new habits. If you are feeling like you are spiralling into your chatty old habits, what you really do need to do are these steps here in action time.

## Action Time

- **Curious Breaths**

You recognise that you are feeling uncomfortable, that you want to chatter over what seems like endless silence.

1. Stop
2. Breathe
3. Observe
4. Assess using THINK PR
5. Learn
6. Thank
7. Breathe
8. Decide

Breaking this down:

1. **STOP**, make yourself stop. Yes, just stop. Shut your mouth even if you must purse your lips together.
2. **BREATHE** a deep, deep breath in through your nose and then out through your mouth. Breathe it slowly just like we did in Chapter 2. Look around and smile at everyone. Just try to look as comfortable as you can. They're probably going to see that you're not quite your usual self and they're going to wonder why you stopped talking. That's okay. Let them wonder. Keep the mystery alive.
3. **OBSERVE** the feelings in your body. Observe what you feel, your heart rate, your stomach, your head, your shoulders, down to the fingertips and your toes. Just observe any areas that are jumping out at you saying, Listen to me. Just see them, feel them. Don't try to change the feelings. Just keep breathing.
4. **ASSESS** what you are about to say before you say it. Is what you are going to say **THINK PR?**

- **True**. Is it truthful? Is it something that comes from a true space?
- **Helpful**. Is it something that's going to be helpful to the people around you to hear what you're going to say?
- **Inspiring**. Don't drag others down? You really want to be positive here.
- **Necessary**. Do you need to say it? Or have you already said it before? Has someone else already said it? Is it something that you think most people already know? For example, the earth is round.
- **Kind**. Is it something that's kind? Do you think that what you're about to say might hurt others? Does it come from a kind space?
- **Professional**. This is a big one for the workplace setting. Does it represent you on a professional plane? Is it something that you should talk about with your friends and not at work? Does it show you to be thoughtful and responsible?
- **Reasonable request**. Is what you are going to ask someone to do, to listen to, a reasonable thing? Or is it something that people would stand back and say, whoa, really, I don't think you should say that. I don't think I should have to do that. That's not even their job or yours.

5. **LEARN**. Having done these things so far, you will have learnt how your body responds to the stress of your spiralling chatter habits. How your body responds to the stopping and the breathing. You're going to learn what it was like to think about what you are going to say. You're going to make the decision to say it or not. That's your learning phase.
6. **THANK** all the behaviour, all the feelings that you have just observed within yourself, pay them respect.
7. **BREATHE**.
8. **DECIDE**. It's time to decide; do you speak, or do you stay silent a little longer and think of something else to say that fits the THINK PR principle?

This is how you stop yourself from spiralling into those old chatter habits. It's going to take some practice and you're not going to get it right the first time. Also, there's going to be a lot of people who will be puzzled by your one-minute silence in conversation. Sometimes I can run this through within ten seconds now that I'm practiced at it, but at first it took me at least a minute or two to go through all steps. I would carry a little card with me that had these steps written on it. This card became my lifeline in social settings, and I would pull it out of my wallet or out of my pocket and just read it. Occasionally I'd sneak to the toilet and hide in a cubicle just to read it, to remind myself of how I needed to reassess my talking habits.

- **Silent Connection**

Learn now how to sit in a comfortable silence with a trusted friend.

I want you to sit opposite one another and look into each other's eyes for one minute.

After each minute one person makes a very brief spoken sentence and then another minute of silence begins again, alternating between you.

Try hard, just to look into each other's eyes. It is a strange sensation, but somehow calming. Connecting with others allows you to sit more comfortably in that silent space. Conversation is no longer necessary.

This is a good exercise to practice your impulse control and to get those listening skills working when your exercise partner is speaking. So, now choose a trusted friend from your list in Chapter 3 and sit with them.

- **Listening**

Ask an open-ended question. By that I mean a question that people cannot just give a one-word answer to. You don't want them to say *yes* or no. For example, you may ask "Do you like dogs?" and their answer may be *yes* or *no*. Instead, ask them what kind of dogs they like and why? Then they must give you a longer answer. The aim is for you to learn something from them.

You want the opportunity to be able to listen. After they've given you their answer, see if you can recall what they've said. Your goal here is to actively listen to their answer in full, without interrupting them, without thinking about what you are going to say next. Just listen to what they have to say.

Then wait for two breaths, or even five, depending on how fast your breathing is right now, because you might be feeling a little anxious. Remember, in through the nose and out through the mouth while you're taking those breaths, that's when you're going to think about your answer. First, you're going to think about what they've said, and then you're going to generate your answer. Don't just fill the space with experiences and things that you've already said before or nuances that you think are going to interest them. Come up with an honest answer that responds to what they had to say. They might say, "I like Greyhounds because they like to go walking, but they're really calm and lazy back at home." So, now you realise they might be a big dog, but they're good in apartments, and you say, "Oh, I didn't know that about Greyhounds." You can even ask, "How did you learn that about Greyhounds?" You're taking interest in something that they have an interest in. They will be happier to answer and continue to converse with you.

This might sound like simple conversation skills. However, for people who tend to be nervous chatters, we don't tend to listen, and we tend to change topics constantly. Forgetting that the first topic might not have been finished. Ending other people's sentences or cutting topics of conversation is not the way to go.

Once you think you've got this listening technique down pat on a one-to-one situation, that is when you start to apply it into a group setting. Start being silent in a group of people and allowing the others to speak and truly listening to what they all have to say until you have a way to respond to them instead of just filling the silent gaps.

## Reward Time

Wow. Take a big breath. You've just reached the end of Chapter 4. Time to give yourself permission to do something nice. Perform a meditation session, even do a bit of yoga, something in another quiet space. Maybe even go for a walk down the beach or sit under a tree. Just observe a little bit of nature for a while. Have some more input other than sound. I'm so proud of you. You need and deserve to reinvigorate your energy levels because you've worked so hard so far. See you in Chapter 5 to energise it.

# Chapter 5

# Energise It

You are working so hard, but it truly feels as though your body, your mind, and your soul need feeding, right?

There are so many things that can get in the way of you being at your best. There's your sleep pattern, regulated by melatonin and your circadian rhythm. This is your internal clock, the 24-hour cycle that your body works within; controlling when you sleep and wake, when you are most productive, even when your body rests and recovers. Everybody's cycle is a little bit different. Many believe it's due to gender or the time and day you were born, others believe it's due to the temperature or the rising and setting of the sun and moon, and so forth. There are so many things affecting your circadian rhythm. With the busy lives that we now live, it's only natural that our body rhythms get off kilter, out of nature's rhythmic sync.

I'm a shift worker, so my rhythm is always a little off. Sometimes I have insomnia, that inability to get to sleep and stay asleep. It's difficult to perform on days when I have had a night with only three hours of interrupted sleep. Other times I have hypersomnia where I want to stay asleep for prolonged periods of time, fifteen hours or more. Working when I'm sleep deprived means I don't operate at my best.

Sleep regulation is in part controlled by sunlight and melatonin, one of those hormones released into the body by the pineal gland. Again, more scientific words, but really all you need to understand is that it helps to keep your core body temperature at its needed levels. Allowing your body to relax and get into sleep mode. Your body temperature must go up and down at contrasting times of the 24-hour day to control your sleep regulation. As a shift working nurse, I can attest that if you don't get enough sun during the day and enough dark during the night, then your sleep patterns are going to be off.

There are other things that can affect your energy level too. For example, your diet makes an enormous difference to creating a healthy body and a healthy mind. We have been told this for centuries… and look, there are endless diet plans on offer that all claim to be the best. Some prefer to go meatless, others low carb, these are only two examples, there are so many choices. Just remember the best diet is a sustainable one, a well-balanced diet that works for you. Put into your basket a balance of all the healthy things you need. There's a theory I heard somewhere about diet that states if you have something of every colour in your diet as well as something of every shape of each organ in your diet, you will become healthier. For example, brown walnuts are great for brain health, and they look like a little brain. Green lima beans they look like kidneys and guess what researchers say they are great for kidney health. So, write yourself a shopping list and commence a great diet before the end of this chapter.

Next is exercise. I can hear you groan. I am not a gym junkie or sports fanatic, but I know it's true that exercise can have an amazing influence on your mood. Here I go again, throwing academic words at you like endorphins and neurotransmitters, dopamine and serotonin. Breaking them all down, when you exercise, you get flooded with good energy, good chemicals that allow you to smile. Relieving the depression, the doom and gloom that's been clouding your brain. So many studies have shown that even the smallest amount of exercise can help keep depression away, reduce anxiety, and even help with a better working memory. Gone are the days when elderly residents were put in a chair in front of the television. I've seen the trend at age care centres around the world that have started introducing exercise sessions for their residents. Glowing results are shown in slowing memory loss and decreases in depression. Even benefits in reducing their decline into conditions like Alzheimer's and dementia.

Sometimes even all the above aren't enough. Even after adding all those things to your routine, you still can't get out of the funk you are in. You are unable to seize and control those ANTs that are driving you deeper and deeper down. If you're anything like the old me, sometimes you think you will never be happy and you think about taking drastic measures. Drastic measures are never the answer, and those are the times to seek a health professional. I spoke to my local general medical practitioner, and he suggested I consider beginning medication. At first, I was against it, I'd tried those ten years previous and hated the way the medication made me feel like an emotionless zombie. But things change and medications are so much different now than they were back in the day. I lowered my resistance to taking meds.

I did a little research and I realised that some medications contained the same things my body couldn't produce enough of to get me over what I needed to get over. For example, SSRI medication, which is a real serotonin hit helped to give me that extra boost that I needed. I couldn't get that extra mental lift without the pills. At the time I was grieving the sudden death of a dear friend and nursing colleague, all the while still coming to terms with the death of my parents and too many close friends over the years to keep count. Working exhausting shifts, I was mega run down. I had no energy in reserve and no time to even prepare a decent diet, let alone to be able to get out for any amount of exercise or sunshine.

By the end of this chapter, you will learn to develop your own plan to get more energy in your life, to brighten your skin and your eyes. Those eyes that have become dull due to a lack of energy. You will rediscover your ability to concentrate and it will increase insurmountably. If you follow the plan, your physical flexibility will increase and the stiffness and pain that you feel every day when you try to get out of bed will be a thing of the past. You'll start to feel healthier and happier because you will no longer be burning the candle at both ends. No more looking in the mirror at a sad, dull skinned, lifeless person. You're going to feel that dreariness fade away and be replaced by a happiness, a brightness. Moisture will return to your dry skin and hair. After bending over to pick something up when it falls to the ground you will just spring up like a child again. I know that's what you want and if you follow this chapter, you can get that all back.

## Story Time

So many times, I made poor lifestyle choices. Just collapsing, watching the television, eating snacks. I really needed to swap those snacks out for something a little bit healthier, more nutritious for my body. But I just craved salty and sweet junk food snacks. More ANTs came to me when I was in my thirties and it said, *'Look at yourself, at those bags under your eyes, you are just so ugly and old.'* I knew I wasn't ugly or at least I hoped I wasn't, I really wanted to believe I wasn't. I wanted to believe I was only tired. I was exhausted every day getting up to endless hectic nursing shift work. Never getting enough sleep, but my ANTs told me I was *'old and ugly'* and I chose to believe them. I had no idea how I was going to overcome this negative mindset until I started at a new gym. I was amazed that the people there were just like me. They had unhealthy habits. They hadn't hopped off the couch for a long time. Many worked long hours and rarely saw the sunlight. They even had pets just like I did, and I must admit my poor dog

## Energise It

never got walked. She sat at the door day after day waiting for me to take her out, but I was getting home and collapsing on the couch with no energy instead.

I wanted to have a new life. I wanted to have energy like everyone on the television and the internet seemed to have. I wanted to have a new body, new mind, those new habits, but I had no idea how to get them. The gym instructors and my new buddies helped me by giving me a recipe plan I could prep once a week. I was already a great good cook and loved cooking, but for some reason I had fallen into the trap of eating processed foods and snacks daily. Having this new plan helped to get me into healthy habits again. I also realised it was tastier then all the junk I had been eating and craving. I was craving sugar and all the disgusting fatty foods. When I replaced them, it only took me a few weeks to realise that the cravings had disappeared, and I was relishing in the taste of fruits and vegetables once again.

I was enjoying eating lean meat, nuts, and a healthier version of crackers, and I didn't have to forego the cheese. These choices meant my digestive system did not have to fight to process what I was consuming. I knew I had heard all this before, but it really was effective when I started small. I cut down the sugar in my coffee from 3 to 2 to 1 and then none. Now I can't even bear to have sugar in a drink at all. It took a few weeks for me to get over sugar cravings and my taste for sugar. I am amazed, even now, how my taste buds adjusted to the lack of sugar.

My mum would have me make a cuppa when I got home from school. I'd make her a milky sweet cup of tea and I would have a sweet milky cup of coffee. Then I became lactose intolerant at the age of sixteen and had to cut out the milk. Within a few months, I barely even noticed I was drinking black coffee. I replaced the milk with a few extra sugars to counteract the bitterness and it was fine. Over the years, the sugars increased from 1 ½ to 2, then all the way up to 3 per cup. That's way too much sugar. Shift working going to sleep at eight in the morning to sleep all day, other days sleeping at two in the afternoon or nine at night or two in the morning. I drank between four and eight cups a day just to cope with the ever-changing shifts. The sugar from those coffees was being stored in my body as fat around my vital organs, and my gut, the muffin top that stopped me looking in the mirror for fear of crying. Not to mention all that caffeine interfering with my sleep.

The first time I went to the gym, I had no idea how hard it was going to be. I got there and I was thinking, wow, my heart rate is sitting so high. It felt like my heart was about to burst out my chest. They told me to slow down, that there was no need to try to run a lifetime of missed of races in one day. "You're over fifty years old, you need to take it easy, just go slow, one step at a time." When I left the gym, I went for a walk with the dog, and I did this every second day. Wow, what a change. Within three weeks, my heart rate came down to a normal level, and every time I exercised I no longer felt as though I was not going to be able to catch another breath.

It was great to bond with the dog again, to walk around and toss the ball. I got in stretches at home because the gym sessions were hard on me at my age. The stretches helped those muscles that, because I hadn't been using them, seemed to have forgotten their job. Yoga stretches, gym, walking the dog, it was intense. I do tend to push myself hard, all or nothing, that's me. You don't have to go that hard, you can start with moderate exercise like a small walk every day before or after work. Even in your lunch break, have your lunch then go for a walk. It'll help you digest your food.

As you learnt in Chapter 2 always set a W.H.A.T. Goals plan and use the Mind Time Cheat technique, and it'll start to feel much easier. Remember that making a regular effort becomes a habit. Habits, when formed will stay with you. I formed habits of sitting for hours on the couch daily and of sleeping for twelve hours on my days off. I changed my sleep pattern, slowly reducing it back to eight hours, then with that extra time in my day, I used it to go for a walk. I cooked that healthy meal at home instead of buying fish and chips or pizza on the way home. It doesn't mean you can never have chips or pizza again; you just get them on your cheat day. It's all in the planning; to achieve anything, you must plan. The traditional health kick, lose weight plans, there's a reason they don't work. Why you bounce straight back and put all that weight back on. You lose your energy, your motivation. They're about denying yourself the things your brain and body loves. Your brain enjoys a treat. Treats are good, but treats are exactly that, just treats.

There was no regularity to my life. How do you stay healthy on that? There have been studies that show shift work can reduce up to ten years of your life. What! That means I could die ten years earlier than I would have if I had not been doing shift work. It's a hard one to reconcile, especially when you're as dedicated to your job as I have been. I have been a shift worker for more than thirty years. I started when I was a teenager working in a kitchen during the Adelaide Grand Prix from 4pm until 4am, scrubbing my fingers to the bone washing dishes by hand. I know you're all laughing right now, *by hand*. The dark ages you say. Dishwashers are the go now, right? Well, we didn't have them in all the kitchens I worked in back then.

It also wasn't a common thing for people to have regular massages for their body to relax. I get a massage every month now, but when I didn't have a lot of cash after my divorce, I would find friends who were just as stressed as me and we would swap out a short shoulder massage for each other. It wasn't a professional massage, but it was better than nothing. It helped to relax my muscles and lower my stress levels. During that time, we would giggle and laugh. The endorphins we got from that, the feel-good hormones, were just as good as going along to a full hour professional massage therapist session. I'd also go for short walks. It doesn't cost anything to go for a walk. I realised how much I could do regardless of my financial constraints. I didn't have to join a gym, but I did need motivation, so I teamed up to walk with friends, and enjoyed that social aspect too. When it became harder and harder to schedule time with friends, I rearranged my finances so as to afford to join a gym.

Now you can even get food boxes delivered to your house, and there's plenty of healthy options. Some of them are already pre-made. It amazes me how it's all come full circle; you can have fruit and vegetables delivered to your house, just like the old days. My dad, when he was living back in the United Kingdom (UK), had a little food delivery van which was all kitted out with vegetable bins. When I was two years old, just before we left the UK to come to Australia, I got inside the van and mixed up all the apples with the potatoes and the pears with the oranges. I just jumbled everything together. My poor dad had to spend ages fixing it all up so he could go on his daily run around the local neighbourhood to sell his wares door to door. Well, now you just order online, and it comes boxed to your door. Fresh with the ingredients and recipes for you to do a quick 10-to-20-minute cook up. I'd sometimes spend an afternoon batch cooking a week of meals to freeze. Then I could take meals to work, reheat dinners at home in the microwave on the busy days when I hadn't had enough rest. It's no different timewise than going down to the tuck shop and waiting fifteen, sometimes twenty minutes for your greasy pizza, or fish and chips to be cooked.

## Discovery Time

**The Five Essentials**

Get yourself moving towards energising your body, mind, and soul.

My keep it easy guide to moderation and balance. Here's what I aimed for and what worked for me.

- **Energising Nutrition**
  8-10 glasses of water daily.
  Foods of all the colours of the rainbow.
  Foods shaped like the organs.
  Minimal processed foods.
  5 food groups Daily Portions:

- 4-6 serves grain/cereal, mostly wholegrain and high in fibre
- 5+ Vegetables, legumes, beans
- 2 Fruits
- 2.5-4 Dairy and alternatives
- 2.5-3 Lean meats like poultry or fish, eggs, tofu, nuts, seeds, legumes, or beans

Low salt
Low sugar
Low fat
Low alcohol
One cheat day a week and only treat foods in small portions and moderation.

- **Easy Body Moving**
  Thirty minutes a day of moderate heartrate increasing exercise. Not all on one day. Space it out over five days in the week. Two days of rest.

- **Restful Sleep**
  6-8 hours over each 24-hour period.
  Sleep preferably at night.
  If sleep is in the day, make it dark, pull the curtains closed, wear an eye mask.

- **Fun vs Work Life Balance**
  Work 5-6 days.
  Work shifts of 7-10 hours a day.
  Play five hours at least 1-2 days a week, and by play, I mean fun, see people, read, get on with hobbies.

- **Chill Out**
  Massage
  Meditate, clear your mind.
  Be in nature.

## Action Time

- **Body Mind Soul Plan**

It's about perspective and it's about how much you care about your own health. Feed your body right and your body will work for you. Sleep right, and your energy level will increase. Exercise more, and happiness will improve, and pain will dissipate. Refer to your free Badass Diary and other printable resources I provide. Save the trees, I suggest you print and laminate the blank plan, then you can fill it out week by week, erase it and start again. You can make a different plan for every week, or you can keep it the same and balance it with that consistency.

How are you going to organise your personal body, mind, and soul plan?

- **Diary Time**

Plan your healthy road to recovery in your Badass Diary. I want you to have fun with it, put in little smiley faces, thumbs up, or gold star stickers. Make it yours. I can guarantee you that if you follow my examples you will start to see an improvement. So many bright, happy stickers than you ever thought possible.

- **Certificate of Achievement**

You'll see your certificate of achievements in your Badass Diary as well. This is where you'll get to note down your daily and weekly successes. Pin them up everywhere around the house. Places where they will encourage you, you can put them on your phone screen saver where you can see them all day. Anywhere you want. It's great to be reminded of the things you've achieved on the inside of your work locker, on your desk, or if you're shy you can put them on the inside of your bedroom cupboard, in your toilet, on your bathroom mirror. Somewhere where it's special for you to be able to see them alone.

It's a congratulations to yourself showing that you are meeting your achievements. You're getting on with your body mind, and soul plan.

## Reward Time

It's time, you've completed Chapter 5, time to jump for joy and do something spectacular for yourself. Go book a facial, a massage, or have a very, very fruity treat or a protein smoothie to get those muscles energised, repaired, and working for you.

Again, well done. Get your teeth into Chapter 6 to learn ways of sorting your time scheduling so you can start to focus more on your goals.

## Chapter 6

# Focus It

Do you feel like life is rushing by so fast that there is never enough time?

Do you find it difficult concentrate with constant distractions interrupting your flow?

Many of us feel that way, I know I do. I've been hearing since childhood that excessive screen usage is detrimental to mental health and in the last few decades, especially since the onset of the COVID-19 pandemic, daily screen time has increased insurmountably. More people are working from home and that involves getting straight on the computer from the moment they get up to the moment they go to bed. They're either on the computer, tablet, mobile phone, or they're on the television. There's overwhelming media distraction everywhere, subconsciously creating stress and worry in our lives.

Pandemic stress and isolation, constant worry, and zero downtime leads to zero relaxation. Now that can't be good for you, can it? You need to get peace and quiet, and comfortable silence back in your life. Switch off those intrusive devices every now and then. With my suggested time management skills, you will gain more enjoyable life moments. Turn back on to the world, people, animals, the nature around you. Shift the attention back on yourself and regain focus on your life path.

Wouldn't you like to be provided with relief from the demands of your time? We have all heard that a stressed mind leads to a sick body. Feeling overwhelmed and unwell is getting you nowhere in life. I call it the device busy syndrome. You wake up and reach for your phone because, well, it is your alarm. On the screen you see the flash of a message awaiting and before your eyes have fully focussed, you are swiping to read. All day there are devices and media bombarding your brain. Flash forward to bedtime where the last thing you look at is the screen as you check your final messages and set tomorrow's alarm. So is the daily cycle, am I right? No one's saying you must give up media, television entirely, especially if it is a part of your job. It's got to be a good thing to plan your time better though. To fit the things you love back into your life by decreasing your dependence time on devices and media.

When your brain receives so much input all the time, it alters your body's chemistry. You feel overwhelmed and stress hormones are released. Many of us just give into the feeling of helplessness and in storms procrastination, getting you nowhere. Those ANTs attitudes of *'Why bother trying, the entire world is'*, to coin a phrase, *'Fucked up'*. I have touched on the stress response before. When fear is triggered; your body creates an intense burst of adrenaline. This leads to you gaining a quick surge of energy. In years gone by, this was to protect us from danger - like a lion coming at us through a field. The body is in full danger mode. The liver dumps sugars into the bloodstream, the lungs expand to allow more oxygen into the blood and the heart pounds to move the oxygen and sugar to the brain and the muscles.

## Focus It

Arms and legs are then powered so that we could run and climb a tree to escape that lion. All those increases in strength, energy, and speed were for a good reason. Even our digestion stops so that all energy can be used for the brain and muscles to get us all the way out of danger. Our pupils dilate so we can see better. Right now, you are living in a world where everything around you, all the devices, busy lifestyle, and media are creating stress and projecting danger to your subconscious mind. Your body is reacting to that. You never get to return to that state of haemostasis, that balance where your body and your mind senses safety. I feel sorry for the subconscious mind never getting any rest. You don't think about it on the surface, and you might not even realise it if I didn't point it out to you.

Then there is another of nature's sabotages that I'm experiencing quite strongly at present. Now that I've hit my fifties, my body just says to me, *'Collapse. Sit on the couch and ignore the world.'* My ANTs tell me *'I'm lazy, all I do is sit on the couch and eat'* and convince me *'I'm going to get fat.'* Well, like many women, it's because of menopause, changes in levels of estrogen and progesterone hormones causing moodiness, fatigue, sugar cravings, foggy brain, and more. It took me a while to work this out, and therefore I encourage you all to be honest with your general practitioners and explain how you're living your daily life. Sometimes there are health life cycles that you hadn't realised were affecting you.

Sometimes there are other things at play like exhaustion from work, raising children and other such things. Men can be affected by hormonal changes too if their levels of testosterone drop too low. There are so many hormonal imbalances that can affect the way you feel, some natural and some not. I've learned not to listen to my ANTs anymore. Because I'm not lazy, I'm proactive. I got treatment and now I am motivated again. I go to the gym, but I just can't help the fact that my body wants to be the shape it is. My body isn't even as bad as my ANTs pretend it is. I am not what I, or even the medical profession, would consider as obese. Like many of you I just look at the magazines and want to be like the twenty-year-old woman I was thirty years ago.

Even with its ever consuming evil, mass media has its benefits in moderation. I learnt it can be helpful if I choose the right positive input. It guides me in looking after myself, others, and the planet. I've discovered some wonderful sources of media out there. If you go and search, you'll find them too. Instead of collapsing into some dreary show that you're not really interested in or browsing endless negative and fake social media pages, get online and search for something else. Put in some positive words, somethings you're interested in. It will take you down a rabbit hole that will lead you to more positive sites. The algorithms can work for you or against you. They are all about giving you more of what you've been looking at and can sell positivity just as easily as negativity. Time to choose the positive route if you must choose media at all. I challenge you to find an escape that brings your mind more peace.

Sometimes I feel like there's no time in the day. I head off from work, and by the time I get home, it's dark and time to go to bed. I have so many creative things I want to do, but it seems like there's never enough time for the things I love. I race around like a chook with its head cut off trying to get a little bit of this and a little bit of that done. Instead of sitting and focusing on one thing at a time, I'm flitting my attention between ten. Somehow, I end up getting nothing completed. I've learned that I can get so much more done when I'm not trying to do everything at once. Its better if I just stop, write a list, and attack each item on the list in order of importance. It's all about organisation and it's about the 80/20 rule, the Pareto principle. The idea that 80% of the effects come from 20% of the causes.[8]

You can achieve more goals if you only put in a little bit of effort at the beginning. Decide on a plan of attack. It feels as though compiling a list might take forever, but it doesn't. It takes two minutes to write one down. Then you can focus on the first item on that list. Before you know it, it's done, and you are on to the next task. If you hadn't made the list, you'd be faffing around aimlessly for double the time. Putting the tasks into focus made your time more productive. By prioritising what you needed to complete, voilà, it helped to use your energy more efficiently. You achieved greater productivity, and got more done in a shorter time frame. It's amazing how much more you can do when you have a plan. Simple!

## 4 P's

Now we come to my four P's - **Planning**, **Prioritising**, **Performing**, and **Pausing**

- **Planning**

You must plan, set those goals, get yourself a to-do list. Having a plan also helps you to minimize procrastination. When you have a clear goal of what you need to get done, you can achieve anything.

- **Prioritising**

Prioritise your time, schedule an appropriate deadline when you want things to be done, and in what order of importance. Do them one at a time.

- **Performing**

It's all about the peak concentrated performance. You must block distraction. You need to avoid multitasking. It's also important to make sure that others respect your time. If they're wasting your time, you're wasting your time.

- **Pausing**

Finally, pausing, you still must schedule downtime breaks. Your body and brain need to have rest as well. If you continue working for ten hours straight, your productivity drops off the further into those ten hours you get. You slow down. You get foggy. It's not the same as it was in the first hour. So, make sure you take regular breaks.

## Story Time

In 2006, when I was thirty-six, I went to live in Japan for a year. I worked as an English Second Language (ESL) teacher. While I was there, I picked up several other jobs. I became an instructor in a nightclub where I taught Salsa, Meringue and Reggaeton dance styles in two languages, English and Spanish. The assistant would verbally translate my lessons on the go into Japanese and Portuguese. I was also a singer in a jazz bar, again in English and Spanish. Now, I don't know how I kept down three jobs, two part-time and one full time, in another country where I barely spoke the language, but somehow, I did.

I had a plan. I knew when I left Australia that I would need to learn some Japanese. I would also need training on the NOVA school teaching style. That was a huge task, but I was committed, I had signed a contract. A few months before I left, I started learning basic Japanese, just enough to get by. Without it even simple things like being able to order food would be a challenge. I pre-arranged transport from the airport to my apartment and my NOVA training time was sorted. With some aid from my new housemates, I quickly oriented myself to the locations containing all that I needed. I set time for myself half an hour a day, to work on the skills I needed. I followed the 4P's.

My plan for this goal had a to-do list. The time was organised. I prioritised it, and I knew I had to have certain things done before the deadline of leaving Australia. When I arrived in Japan I didn't want to be stuck missing trains to my apartment because I hadn't done my research. There was a definite necessity to meet this deadline. I took myself away to my room and locked the door. I concentrated on studying the language with headphones on so no one could interrupt me. I had to avoid getting distracted by other things. I found myself procrastinating, multitasking, tidying my room. So I switched it up and went to the park. I sat on my own, staring at the river, learning the language with the headphones on. It was easier not to get distracted without other people around and my belongings out of sight. I also ensured that I had downtime, short breaks. I only did my studies for half an hour at a time because anything more and my brain would fade. I'd lose concentration and start to struggle; my ANTs would creep in, and I would beat myself up. *'Oh, you're not getting this, try harder! Are you stupid, a 5th grader would get this!'* But really, all I needed to do was take a break. A pause to have water and food for energy.

Once I arrived in Japan, I had a week to learn my surroundings, my new job, and how to get to wherever I was going. The training was intense, but I made it through, again, with the same goal-setting techniques. Of course, it was a lot easier to avoid distractions because when I got home from work and turned on the television, I didn't understand a word they were saying. There were no translated subtitles, so I was television-free for most of the year. Mind you, it didn't stop my brain trying to understand the advertisements that were plastered all over the trains, subways, and buses. Even the sides of the buildings were lit up with ads, but they were in Japanese too. I thought it was a low-key stress, not something that would distract me. I hadn't considered that I was in sensory overload, which was just as exhausting. I got used to this though, after the first month or two. Eventually every train ride was a relaxing trip home in silence.

## Discovery Time

How are you going to get your media 'time out'?
Can you make yourself a plan to decreasing your sensory overload time?

Think about how many hours a day you are on your computer, tablet, mobile telephone, etc.
How much do you watch your TV or other media devices?
What about listening to music?
Tally up how many hours that takes up in your day.

Remember your body needs other things too.
You need eight hours to sleep,
a few hours to ready yourself- shower, dress, prep and eat your food.

Then to travel to work and survive a shift.
How much time does that leave you to exercise, socialise, relax, to just zone out, allowing your body, your mind to recover?
How does this differ on your days off work?
With how your time is organised now, are there enough hours in the day for it all?

## Action Time

Stopping the overwhelm now, it's Badass Diary time to sit down and put each of those twenty-four hours into perspective. To design the lifestyle you want and deserve.

- **Lifestyle Planner**

Each week you are going to spend five minutes reassessing your schedule. You won't need to do this forever, just until you form new habits. Then use it occasionally as a great tool to see what is missing if you slip back into old habits.

Starting with the essentials, write out your plan of how you are going to spend your time each day this week.

Allocate an amount of time to each item listed:

>    Sleep
>    Work and transportation
>    Food shopping, preparation, and consumption
>    Personal care i.e., showering, shaving, makeup.
>    Rest and relaxation
>    Exercise and nature
>    Socialising with family, friends, pets.
>    Non-work media time. For example, mobile phone, games, music, tv, books.

Make sure that you are including some fun things and add them to make this 24-hour list your own. Do you have any hobbies? Do you have family or friends that you are intent on keeping contact with? Make sure you add them to your own individual list so you can prioritise them.

- **Long View Goals**

Back in Chapter 2, we talked about the things that you would tell your younger self to do if you knew you could not fail.

Now is the time to start planning those in your Badass Diary.

Look at the long view page and follow this 5-step guide:

1. Start with one big W.H.A.T goal/dream to achieve in a year.
2. Think about what you need to complete in the first six months to be halfway to this achievement.
3. Break down all the steps you must achieve to get to the six-month mark. Set up to three smaller monthly goals.
4. Decide on up to six small tasks a week to get you to each of the monthly goals.
5. Lastly, incorporate these six tasks into your lifestyle planner above.

Look again at your one-year end goal.

Breaking it down into smaller parts allows you to see the goal as achievable.

- **5 Breaths, 5 Sensations to Mind Central**

There's a short mindfulness exercise that I find helpful to centre myself in the morning, although it can be done at any time of the day. By feeling aware of your surroundings in a positive way you can relax. Reminder, you are going take nice deep breaths in through the nose and out the mouth.

1. **Breathe** in deep and hold it for five seconds.
2. **Release** it, breathing out slowly for ten seconds.
3. **Drop** your shoulders and relax your muscles with each breath out
4. **Concentrate** while you're breathing out, observe one thing you can **see**. For example, while sitting here, I can see the bird on the tree in my garden through the window.
5. Next breath, one thing you can **hear**. For example, I can hear the dog's nails tapping as she walks on the wooden floor.
6. Next breath, one thing you can **taste**. For example, I can taste a metallic taste in my mouth. Just observe. Don't drift into thoughts like 'because I haven't had enough water.'
7. Next breath, one thing you can **smell**. For example, I can smell the freshness of the rain that's coming down right now.
8. Last breath, one thing you can **feel**. For example, I can feel the arm of the chair, its solid and hard, but smooth.

Now it's your turn. Five breaths, five sensations, what do you **see, hear, taste, smell** and **feel**?

Mindfulness helps start your day concentrated and focused.

## Reward Time

I am so proud of you.
Are you proud of yourself?
You should be!
You are choosing to try new things.

Choose something to celebrate now you have reached the end of Chapter 6. You could do something creative, listen to your favourite music. Have a little dance in the rain.

Go and get to it. Achieve your goals and smash through your habitual avoidance behaviours. Turn the page to Chapter 7; and while some would say, "Ready or not," I would say, "I know you're ready to face Chapter 7."

# Chapter 7

# Face It

This is where we get to the nitty gritty of what to do when your ANTs overwhelm you triggering your out-of-control stress responses. There are lots of questions to face here! Take them one at a time and breathe.

How do you respond to stress?
Do you fight, flight, freeze or fawn?
What do those terms mean?

Are you one of those people who goes into a space of avoidance?
What's your go-to behaviour when your ANTs leave you feeling so overwhelmed that you don't even know where to start?
Do you jump into escapism, wishful thinking, or daydreaming?
Do you bury your emotions?

Are you a self-isolationist?
Are avoiding gatherings and using procrastination behaviours on a regular basis. Cancelling last minute, not answering calls or texts from people? Avoiding places so that you can feel safe?
Do you collapse in front of the TV or just head to bed and sleep?

Avoidance is your brain's way of helping you escape tricky situations or thoughts. Again, it's your brain's way of dealing with what it perceives as danger. This can be damaging to your relationships, your career, and your own self-esteem. You can create obsessive behaviours; those unwanted ideas running through your head causing you to react on impulse in persistently continuous repetitive ways. They become compulsive as you try to relieve your anxiety, negative emotions, and thoughts.

What are your strongest behaviours that you use to escape impulses?
Do you run from things or become the centre of attention?
Do you endlessly chatter?
Do you turn to vices like coffee, food, nicotine, alcohol, drugs, or even sex?
Or do you just go into denial that there even is a problem?
Do you distract yourself, and put everything off until tomorrow, a tomorrow that never ever comes?

Maybe you do them all at various times in response to different triggers, leaving you feeling like you have no control over your life. Unfortunately, a lot of these reactions don't help you to settle your ANTs. There are solutions, techniques that can help you to lower your stress levels. To be more in control of your stress responses, your compulsive actions, and your life.

If you don't do these now, the repetitive damage to yourself and your relationships will just continue to grow with the embarrassment and shame around your behaviours. The ANTs you have running around inside your head will breed and multiply. At first your vices feel amazing, but it doesn't take long to crash back down and listen to those ANTs again. There is a reason for this and it's not entirely your fault. When you do something that makes you feel good, your body releases Dopamine, a feel good hormone. When you stop indulging in your vice, your dopamine levels reduce. You crash back down, dropping into levels of tiredness, moodiness, and even depression. Your brain wants you to get back to the happy feeling. So, the cycle begins. You throw yourself back into your addictive vices.

I know it's easy to keep clinging to these behaviours because it's the only way you know how to cope. I mean, you've spent a lot of time developing your own behaviours. Well, it is your time now to make changes. You must make the decision to change. Yes, it's taking a risk. Take a chance so that you can change your life. You have a lot to gain. It's all about the 3 Cs; Choices, Chances, Changes.

## Story Time

Whenever my mood was low, I gave into my sugar cravings. I could eat an entire bag of lollies in five minutes, and it made me feel great. For a brief time. It was just the released dopamine, that burst of happy energy. I'm perimenopausal, meaning that my estrogen and progesterone levels are sometimes high, other times low, affecting my sugar cravings, fatigue, my mood swings. I could see my body was, while trying to help me, sabotaging me at the same time. All this sugar took a toll on my waistline. My body-confidence plummeted. It wasn't helped by partying like there was no tomorrow, numbing my brain and body with copious amounts of alcohol on every day off.

Since my late teens, my vices included drinking to excess, which often lead to a variety of sexual encounters. I desired to feel noticed and appreciated. I wanted to feel loved, valued, important. Obviously, this did not work out as I had hoped. I woke up each morning after a night out with a headache and hangover. Often not knowing where I was, how I had gotten there, and lying next to someone whose name I couldn't remember. My ANTs shouted at me, '*I hate that I need this. I just can't stop myself. I have no control.*'

On one occasion, in my late forties, I was on a night out with friends, and they introduced me to a nice young guy. We continued drinking cocktails. My friends thinking the whole time I was A-okay because, as they put it, I could "really hold my alcohol." I have a tipping point though. I go from seeming as though I'm fine, happy, and tipsy, to throwing up in the toilet. Provided I was not at that tipping point, everyone was under the impression I was fine to make my own decisions. At one stage in the night, I got in an uber. I don't even remember getting in it. Somehow, I took this young guy home, and to be honest, it was all a blur, the things we did were also blurred. I woke up the next morning with him poking me awake asking where the toilet was.

I had no idea what his name was. I could barely even remember meeting him the night before. I directed him to the toilet telling him he'd have to put on his jeans because I had housemates who didn't need the shock of a naked man prancing about. When he lifted his jeans, everything fell out of his pockets. There was the most ungodly sound of coins, cards and his wallet hitting the wooden floor. Both our heads were pounding. He didn't worry about trying to pick it all up, instead he left and made his way to the toilet. While he was gone, I was racking my brain trying to remember his name. Nope, it wasn't coming to me. I looked down at the mess on the floor and saw his driver's license. Eureka! I picked it up, but it was too blurry to read. I couldn't find my glasses, so I grabbed my phone. I don't know how I thought of that when I was so hungover, but I took a photo of it and increased the size of the photo until I could read his name. Oh, okay, now I knew what to call him when he came back.

I don't know if any of you have ever had this kind of experience. I suffered from such shame. I was worried. I had just created more anxiety for myself, wondering if we'd been safe with the sex, wondering if I needed to pop to the general practitioner for a STD test. I knew I couldn't get pregnant. I didn't have a uterus anymore, so that worry was at least out of the way. My ANTs ran rampant again. *'You are so stupid. Why couldn't you just stop at one drink?'* At the time, I didn't know why I couldn't stop, I thought I was just having fun. I tried to excuse my behaviour, telling myself, *'It's okay, you have managed to pick up some gorgeous young guy who's almost half your age. It's fine. Just boast about it to your friends and make yourself feel better.'* And that's what I did, I bragged to all my friends. Living in a small city, I wasn't going to reveal his name, so I just said, "This cougar picked up and it was a great night." I couldn't even remember the night, but somehow, I convinced everyone it was awesome, and I was living a wonderful lifestyle. But deep down inside I was depressed, I was anxious. I was not living my best life. It was important for me to start making better choices, safer choices.

There are many ways that our avoidance behaviours can step in to protect us from threats or traumas. They can be situation-based. For example, when I was twenty, I was traumatically gang raped in the home of people I knew and trusted. The perpetrators were never charged, and for over twenty years my ability to go back to the same neighbourhood was completely decimated. I was diagnosed with PTSD (post-traumatic stress disorder). Afterwards, not only could I not go back to that neighbourhood, but I also had trouble looking anyone in the eye, especially if they looked anything like my attackers. I had trouble being in small spaces with others; elevators were a nightmare. Being alone in rooms with others, even people I knew, sent my head in a spin. Catching the bus, *hell*, even walking out my front door was sometimes near impossible.

I had also developed what's called cognitive avoidance. My subconscious convinced me to not think about those things. I distracted myself. I would go off into a fantasy world. People thought I was a vague daydreamer, but in reality I was disassociating. The internal conscious working of my brain was shutting down going on autopilot to protect me, so I didn't have to face the pain. I became a chronic worrier, and everything became about *'What if this'* and *'What if that.'* These worries became obsessive. At other times I would substitute different feelings for the ones I was avoiding. Instead of feeling scared, I would get angry. When absolutely overwhelmed with my feelings, I would get confrontational. I would lash out at some of my best friends, telling them to just leave me alone. Often, I'd tell them "I'm fine" then I'd get up and dance, sing a song, become the centre of attention and happiness just to cover my pain.

This is when I would turn to all my vices, all those substances. I hit the bottle, the sex, the junk food. I hit anything I could get my hands on to make me feel better, even if for only a fleeting moment. Hell, I even started smoking cigars for a while after my parents died. They both died of smoking related diseases so me smoking made absolutely no sense at all. I threw myself into avoidance techniques like cleaning obsessively around the house or relying on lucky charms or talismans. I was creating endless rituals to increase my sense of safety, some of which also made no sense. I would get a packet of colourful lollies, like jellybeans for example, and would sit and put them in order of their colours. Then count them and order the colour groupings from highest to lowest. Then I would eat them in that order. This OCD made no logical sense, but I was a girl possessed. So I could avoid feeling my anguish I organised things.

For the first few months after the gang rape, I avoided people altogether. I avoided events, I avoided my friends, and there was no way I was going to have sex again. I told myself, and believed, I would never ever fall in love again. Whenever I was attracted to someone, I got that tingly, rapid heart racing feeling of butterflies, and instantly started spiralling into a state of panic. My brain confused it as the same feeling that I had with the intensity of the sexual assault. That was my somatic avoidance , my physical anxiety, stress response brought on by my past trauma.

There are few distinct types of avoidance, and I went through them all at one stage or another. With a lot of assistance, I managed to get my avoidance techniques under control, but not before my ANTs had built another home in my mind; one of regret, and they undermined my confidence. *'How could I put myself in harm's way, I should have known they were bad people. I am too trusting.' 'I am never going to be capable of being in a successful relationship.' 'I can't even go out on my own to catch bus, I won't ever be safe.'*

I fell deeper into a state of depression and anxiety, I had a tug of war relationship with my sense of control. Sometimes I had a false sense of control where I believed I could do anything, be anything. At other times, my ANTs would convince me that I couldn't control anything in my life. I had social anxiety and panic disorders. I'm an extrovert and I had moments where I didn't want to be around people at all. This was opposite to my natural personality. I was trying intensely to decrease my anxiety and prevent my obsessive fears from coming true. I thought I was creating a place of comfort and control for myself. I was just creating more problems. I eventually made the smart choice to find a mentor, a support person, someone who could understand and diagnose what I was going through. I needed help to replace these trauma-response behaviours with healthier ones. I had a lack of self-awareness of my own behaviours for many years. Well no more. As my father used to say, "Don't put off until tomorrow what you can do today." He'd say, "Girl, it will be like a thousand mosquitoes buzzing in your brain from now until you sort things out. That's just going to be loud and painful as they buzz around and sting inside your skull." A wise man was my father.

## Discovery Time

Earlier in the book I touched on fight, flight, freeze, and fawn. I tended to be mostly fawn or fight back in the day and sometimes I still am. This is a good time to explain to you the differences between the 4 F's: Fight. Flight. Freeze. Fawn.

- **Fight vs Flight**

When you feel as though you can overpower or overcome a threat, your hormones and responses set you up to win that fight. You and your muscles are ready to go. You feel the need to punch, stomp, kick or even speak out in a loud angry voice. Most people get a knot in their stomach, tightening of their jaw, grinding of their teeth. There can be an intense feeling of anger and you want to yell, scream, or roar, let your inner lion loose. That's the fight.

But when you feel as though you can't overcome that danger or threat, you go into flight mode. More hormones, adrenaline mostly, will give your body what you need, that burst of energy to run, to go. You feel like you must get away. Your pupils dilate so you can see better, and your eyes might shoot around from side to side, and up and down. You can't steady yourself. There's a numbness in your arms and legs, but you are constantly moving, and legs and feet and arms are restless, fidgety. You might feel tense or trapped. This is the flight, you're ready to spring and take off.

- **Freeze vs Fawn**

Both are when you feel as though you're stuck and can't escape You can't fight, and you can't flight. A sense of dread comes over you. You go pale, you feel stiff, a bit cold and numb. Your heart rate decreases, and yet it pounds immensely, it's loud. This is the freeze. You don't move, you just stand there quiet, silent, in a state of dread. Hoping the threat will pass you by.

Then there is the fawn. This is the 'fake it to make it' coping mechanism. When again, you can't fight or flight, but the freeze isn't really something you can do either. You become very agreeable, very people pleasing. All you want to do is make other people happy, to distract them. You get extremely helpful, appeasing to deescalate the situation. That's your way of getting out of there, eventually.

## Action Time

I just kept telling myself it would be easier to face it when I was prepared and ready. Really! All I needed to do was stop kicking and screaming, loosen up and let it all out. The time to act is *now*.
Now it's time for you to act.
Badass Diary time!

- **Easy Self-Validation**

Help yourself validate the feelings you have. Understand them, acknowledge them, and let them be. Don't fight them. This is your rational mind helping your emotional mind, exorcising its demon ANTs.

*Acknowledge it*! The feeling you're feeling, you need to acknowledge it. For example, I feel anxious, my heart is racing, my head feels fuzzy.

*Allow it*! Be with that feeling, just allow it to be there. Breathe, don't allow it to overwhelm you. Just let the feeling sit there. For example, it's okay to feel anxious.

*Understand it*! Get curious about the feeling you're having, strive to understand it. Ask why? It makes sense that I feel anxious when I go to the neighbourhood where I was raped. The place reminds me of that intense event that harmed me physically and mentally. My feelings are protecting me from a danger that is no longer there.

- **Settling Your Emotion**

Choose an ANT, one that would normally trigger you into your avoidance behaviour. It's time to understand your body's reaction to this ANT. Choose a safe, quiet place to do a body scan.

**Breathe** deep in through your nose, and starting from the top of your head, scan your attention down to your fingertip and then down to your toes. Notice every sensation in your body with each breath.
Does your head pound?
Is your face hot?
Does your chest feel tight?
Do your fingers tingle?
Any sensation you note, just let it be. Allow your body to feel what it feels and simply observe it very closely.

**Next**, with another deep breath, you are going to do a thoughts and emotions scan. What ANTs and emotions come up?
Do you feel silly, angry, tired?
What thoughts and emotions are your ANTs not allowing you to process?
Go with that feeling and breathe. Recognise it, acknowledge it, observe it, and be kind to yourself. It is okay to feel these feelings and think these thoughts. Breathe.

**Repeat** the exercise several times until you can note down in your Badass Diary what the thoughts, emotions, feelings, and sensations were.

**Read** them back to yourself. Imagine you are reading the journal given to you by a friend. What would you say to that friend about their body scan? Remember, be as kind to yourself as you would be to a good friend.

- **Problem Solving**

**What** is the threat or problem ANT you thought about in the previous exercise?
**Imagine** how you solve it.
**Believe** you have the resources to cope.
**Write** down as many ways as you can to overcome this threat.

You have the resources. You just need to unlock them.

Next, it's time to put those ANTs, those threats, where they belong. In the rear-view mirror, right?

**Imagine** you are looking up at the sky.
There are many clouds up in the sky, and within one cloud imagine the ANTs you've written on the page.

**Problem solve.** Now imagine your solution to solving those ANTs, those threats.
Write it down in your mind's eye, on a gust of wind.
Re-read your solution, believe it will work.

**Clear it** as you watch this gust of wind blow that cloud away.
As the cloud drifts off further and further into the distance and dissipates, so too do the intense feelings throughout your body along with the emotions.

- **Cost-Benefit Analysis**

To help motivate you to make changes in your life, create two pros and cons lists for behaviours and vices you want to change.

**The first list** is the pros and cons for not changing, for continuing your behaviour or vice.
**The second list** is a pros and cons list for what happens when you change the behaviour or vice.
**No more avoidance**; the definitive answer on making change should now be clearer.
**Create** your list of behaviours, vices to change.
**Plan** using your tools and get to changing.

You've got this!

# Reward Time

You've worked hard in this chapter. Give yourself permission to do something nice. Go fruit picking, fishing, lie under a tree and look up at the sky listening to the birds.
You've finished Chapter 7, who are you going to share your achievements so far with?

Let me help you continue to develop your core trusty egg people in Chapter 8.

# Chapter 8

# Share It

Community, friendships, relationships, why are they so important for our wellbeing? When we connect with others we expand our thinking, our knowledge, our universe. Without community, there is an intense feeling of social isolation and loneliness, which often leads to illnesses such as heart disease, addiction, depression, anxiety, and even self-harm. Finding our tribe, or more often tribes, is such a crucial step in the healing journey. Linking with like-minded people while still being open to change is one of the most human qualities that helps us to thrive. One of the many important roles of oxytocin, another hormone, is to help us relate to others. To feel a connection and a trust. It helps us to be empathetic, and it increases during sexual arousal, which allows us to bond with our partners.

Are you an introvert or an extrovert? This can make an enormous difference in how you relate to others. Extroverts gain vibrancy and energy while socialising in larger groups, while introverts need more alone time or smaller group encounters to feel energised. Regardless of which one you are, you can still gain belonging, acceptance, and connectivity within the world. You can learn to have love for and to accept love from others. Most importantly, to accept and have love for yourself. Without it, your loneliness will grow, and your self-worth will continue to plummet. You disconnect when you don't feel you deserve a place in the lives of others, or in the community as a whole. It's then that depression can often follow.

## Story Time

During my school years I listened to all the bullies. My ANTs picked up their cruelty crumbs and carried them onward, saying, *'You're worthless, unlovable. Who'd want to be your friend anyway?'* At first, I just cried. Then other times I went home and patted the dog, gave my mum a hug. I did anything but talk about it to anyone. Eventually I tried to fight back at these bullies, I started by saying, "Well, I don't want to be your friend anyway." I'd sit alone at lunch, no one around to talk to because they were all off with the popular kids. One day I looked around and I saw another girl sitting on a bench by herself. Someone had thrown her lunch down on the ground and she was just crying, looking at it. I walked over, I helped her pick it up. She was stunned and said, "What are you doing that for?" And I just couldn't understand why she was puzzled, I thought it was natural to help someone in distress. She stopped crying, and we sat down and talked. We realised we were both the same; we both felt worthless and undervalued…well, until that moment. We made a friendship and now had each other.

Every lunchtime we looked around and saw the popular kids kicking the football, playing kiss chasey, eating their lunches, laughing, dancing around. They looked so happy, and we were still miserable.

## Share It

Even though we had each other, we couldn't understand why they didn't want us. The ANTs were in control of the kingdom in our brains. This girl turned out to be one of my closest friends through the whole of primary school. When we went our separate ways to different high schools, it was heartbreaking, but years later we reconnected on Facebook and went out to a concert together. It felt like old times, but we'd both come so far from those old days.

Starting high school was beginning from scratch all over again, trying to find my fit into a much bigger realm. Once again, I found myself sitting silently, eating by myself on the oval at lunch, watching the cool kids do their thing. Many of them brought the friendships they'd forged in primary school with them to high school. And there I was, alone, separated from my one good friend. I hoped since I did it once, I could do it again—build a friendship, just one. In marched the ANTs with, *'Who'd want to be your friend anyway?'* I sat there silent. I don't know how many weeks I sat without really making any real connections. I went to class after class. I tried to be the centre of attention, make jokes to be popular. Sometimes it worked, sometimes it didn't. I knew how to talk because, remember, I was a great conversationalist, but somehow, I just hadn't found another person I could relate to. I was this little brown girl in a school filled with mostly white kids who only saw my skin colour, my afro hair. When they got to know me only then I was cool, fun. But I had to keep that cool and fun persona going and that was exhausting.

Ugh I realised, I only had worth when I wasn't being myself because *'Who'd want to be my friend anyway?'* Gee, thanks ANTs. Along the way, I involved myself in things that I liked. I studied drama for my first two years in high school because I loved to perform. I made a few friends there. I wasn't particularly confident in my performances, but I loved it. In year 12, I was invited to be part of the State Rock and Roll of Eisteddfod Competition by the director. One of the girls who had continued doing drama through to year 12 was directing the show for her end of year final grade. You see, my parents decided that drama was not a substantial career for a young lady to get into, that it would never lead to anything. So, from year 10, I was pulled out of drama and put into more academic classes. When I was chosen to be in the Eisteddfod as an extracurricular venture I jumped at the chance. I got to be a skeleton on stage where I jumped and danced around. I loved it. I decided that when I finished high school, after starting a 'real' career, I would go and find a way to perform somehow. Even if my parents didn't approve, even if I was no good, I'd find a way because I really loved it.

By the time I left high school, I had a white shirt signed by so many of my fellow students and even some of the teachers. Kids I didn't even know were signing my shirt. Most kids have yearbooks for signing these days, but I valued that shirt because it was given to me by my father. Gradually, through my school years, I'd become one of the cool kids. I had no idea how because I still didn't see myself as a cool kid. I have been lucky enough to maintain contact on and off with some of the best people I met in high school, and I cherish those friendships. A few have grown closer since the death of my family and have become my new chosen family and have spent many events, Birthdays, Christmases, etc, together.

It all began again, leaving high school and starting a new job, having to build new friendships. I was sick of this transition. I now realise it is just how life is meant to be, a series of transitions. No matter what happens, every time I had to try and build new friendships, the ANTs would be there convincing me I was worthless. Repeating endlessly, *'Who'd want to be your friend anyway?'* In time I met my husband. We got married but twelve years later we got divorced. Overnight, so many of the friendships I'd made over those years vanished, leaving me completely lost and alone, unable to squash those ANTs.

Then, within four months of my separation, my mother died. My father died when I was twenty-six and now my mother when I was thirty-three. I was orphaned. I wasn't a child, but I felt like one. I had no brothers or sisters, no contact with extended family abroad. My parents came to Australia, the land of opportunity, by themselves.

## Share It

A place where they could work hard and finally afford to own their own home, and provide me with good schooling and they hoped, a bright future. All my adoptive relatives, aunties, uncles, cousins, they didn't immigrate with my parents and me. I had only briefly met a few of them on a one-month trip around London and Scotland so they were barely more than strangers I hadn't connected with them. I found myself in an immense state of grief and shock with few friends and no connection to family.

I picked myself up and started building a new pool of friends again. I finished my university course, and I travelled to Japan for a year to work as an ESL teacher for a private language school. I was following the boyfriend I had at the time. When I got there, our romantic relationship collapsed. Stubborn and committed, I stayed the entire year of my work contract. That year, in that job, was one of the best years of my life to date. I made new friends and started to get some of that confidence I was desperately needing, and all in another country on the other side of the equator from home. At first, I could barely speak any of the Japanese language, yet I still managed to make friends.

It turns out I'm quite charismatic. I didn't know how I got that way at first, but after much thought I realised it was from those childhood years of trying so hard to impress people. I had learnt techniques in communication that worked. Once I had an in with that communication, I was able to show people more of my true self. Surprising to me, they liked me. It seemed a shame to leave behind my new friends from my time in Japan, but I'm grateful we discovered ways to stay in contact over the years. As the tools on social media have grown, so have my friendships with people from my travels around the world.

Coming back home to Australia was a little easier than leaving. I had a community of friends that I had maintained contact with. I reconnected with them face to face. Over time, friends came and went, and I kept learning to adapt. I looked for people with similar values to me, my tribes. Kind people were added to my life to create a beautiful calming rock pool around myself.

## Discovery Time

What is love?
What does it mean to be a faithful friend, a family member?
An acquaintance in the wider community?

As I see it, love's a feeling, a sense of belonging and it drives behaviours of kindness, of honesty and trust. I don't understand the contrived idea of unconditional love held by the media and wider community at large. I see this as some cruel myth. There are plenty of children out there who are told their parents are supposed to love them unconditionally. What happens when they don't? They throw their children to the wolves the moment that their child's values don't match theirs. Friends of mine in the LGBTIQ+ community have not spoken with family members since coming out. Parents, children, brothers, sisters, having no contact for years all because of who they love or how they live their lives. So, unconditional love; I don't believe it, I don't trust it. I think you create your own tribe of loved ones around you, the people who show you that they care. When you let them in, they let you in. When it comes down to it, it's all about making the effort, and investing the time in yourself and in others.

Don't get me wrong, every now and then I get down on myself and I think no one cares. My ANTs didn't go away, they still tell me, *'You're such a loser and who'd want to be your friend anyway?'* We all live busy lives and sometimes I still feel alone. But I counter that feeling with simple tools that encourage me to push past my ANTs and thrive. No longer do I burn out trying to do everything for myself. I've found others to relate to in my life, others just like me. Similar fears, interests, and a longing to unite and create our own strong communities.

Just remember, your thoughts only live in your mind. Sometimes you think when your friends haven't called you in months that they don't have time for you, that they never think about you and don't really care about you. Just remember, you can pick up the phone too. What's stopping you? It's quite possible that you and your friends are all thinking the same thing as you and your friends have things in common, ANTs in common, too. Remind yourself that if you're busy, they're probably busy too. They have families, they have jobs, they have hobbies. They are not at your disposal; they're not each individually going to be there all the time. That's why you need a community to fulfill your varied friendship needs.

## Action Time

Invest time in finding your people, your circle of family and friends. Those who support each other and encourage you to be the best badass you they believe you can be. Create drawings in your mind like my rockpool. This is where you are going to visualise placing all the new friendships and some of the old ones, as you create a community around you.

- **Think or Swim, a Visualisation Exercise.**

Rivers are amazing forces of nature. When a river is frozen, living plants and animals within it hibernate. When it doesn't flow, it festers and stagnates, nothing healthy can survive. When a river flows freely, it can sustain life. Flowing through rockpools and into dams, creating power for our communities. Strong rivers create new pathways to nourish the land. It's time to create a flowing pathway to your strong community.

Close your eyes. Imagine you are in a river. It's a big river and there's a moderate current, just strong enough to take leaves and branches down river as they fall in. Around you are all the people in your life.

First, I want you to single out your acquaintances. People who, for example, are work colleagues, or you met at a club. You may not know each other very well but they are kind and gentle and it's nice to have them cheering you on from the sidelines. Those people swim ever so gently to the riverbank. They climb up and they walk along the bank of the river waving to you from a distance. Occasionally they'll swim out, give you a little bit of sustenance, and then swim back to the

## See You Reclaim You Be You

bank. There they walk along, just within your sight. These are your outer circle friends, your acquaintances.

Next, I want you to think about the people in your life that are challenging to be around. Sometimes they are difficult to bear, but you feel a responsibility to them. You feel they are holding you back. Don't let them weigh you down. Swim upriver just a little and let them be taken with their weight down-river and out to sea. Let the emotional weight that they carry wash away.

And now finally you swim to a warm, calm rock pool. Towards your tribe of close friends. The ones that boost you, make you feel happy. Support you and want so much to see you succeed. Splash around happily in that river rockpool with them.

Open your eyes. Who did you see in each of those places?

That's who you're going to put in on your tribe chart. This is your community. These are the people that are going to help you thrive through life. Now, go build that community. Be you extrovert or introvert, build your rockpool as big or as small as you need.

- **Creative Affirmations**

"But Donna, you say, what about me?" It's time to see you. Grab that mirror and start working on self-love. Hold that mirror up and investigate yourself. You've done it before in Chapter 1, but this time you're going concentrate on boosting your self-esteem.

Every time an ANT comes into your brain, you are going to squash it with a positive affirmation. Don't believe the ANTs. You're going to fight back, challenge them, squish them, spray them. Do anything you can to kill those ANTs. It's not about anger, it's about love. To the ANTs that say *'You are worthless, mean, stupid'* remind them that the old you may have listened, but the new you has new tools. You are worthy of more; you are definitely worthy of love, self-love. You are going to reclaim your worth from your ANTs. Create your own affirmations that work to counteract the individual ANTs within your own brain. For example, *'I am loved,' 'I am kind,' 'I am smart.'*

This is a lifelong journey, and it gets easier as time goes on; practice definitely makes perfect. On the inside and the outside, every single one of you is perfect. For some of you, that would've been a difficult exercise. I know it was hard for me. It took me a long time to do these exercises, and to believe the positive affirmations. It takes repetition. You need grit, to quieten those ANTs. I finally did squish my *'Who'd want to be your friend anyway?'* I countered it with the overconfident response of, *'Plenty of people because I am loved, let me list them for you…'* and I kept adding to my list as I created friendship bonds. Of course, when I started, I didn't believe the affirmations, but daily, I wrote this down and I read it often. I faked it until I made it my reality, my new truth. It worked. I wish that we had all been taught to do this from day one, when we were born. Throughout school and onward in life. I wish there were advertisements on the television reminding us that we are, each one of us, someone of great worth.

## Reward Time

You've finished Chapter 8, celebrate! Go on a bonding outing with one of your core rockpool people. Go and sit on a real rock, throw pebbles into the water, and see which of you has the best throwing arm. They probably give the best hugs too. But remember:

*"If you can't love yourself, how in the hell are you gonna love somebody else?"*[9]

Now,

*'Good luck and don't fuck it up."*[10]

Look at you, getting ready to own your future with your community of supporters. See you in Chapter 9.

# Chapter 9

# Own It

Do you often find yourself thinking in circles and getting nowhere?
Are you incessantly worrying about the future?
Looping is getting stuck in a form of repetitive thought or worry pattern, leading you to overwhelming emotions about these thoughts. You try to pre-empt future troubles. Sometimes you act out, solving nothing. Then you move back into the worry again. Worrying about the actions you are yet to make. So, on goes the loop.

Do your thoughts live in the past, worrying about what you could have, would have, or should have said or done?
Do you end up living with guilt and self-blame?
This is different, it's called ruminating, which is getting stuck in negative thoughts or worries of the past and only the past.

There are significant changes you will feel in your life when you stop ruminating and looping. You get to live in the here and now. Stop blaming yourself for every little thing that goes wrong. Limit your catastrophising and calm those ANTs of yours. If you don't calm these thoughts, you end up in a self-loathing pattern that just digs deeper into your self-worth, your self-love. I talked in the last chapter about the necessity to love yourself. Essentially, if you don't love yourself and others, then you fall into intense sadness, negativity.

Many people slide the slippery slope into depression and anxiety. All the self-loathing brought about by ANTs can also feed so much on your brain. The effects of anxiety and depression can be wide reaching. They have an intense effect on your immune system. Your immune system is necessary to keep you at a healthy mental and physical state, to be able to function from day to day.

## Story Time

I fell into a deep dark hole countless times before applying the tools I share in this book. I have heard people talk about a fog, a dark cloud hanging over them or a black dog looming around. For me, it wasn't like that. For me, it was not being able to see colour. I walked outside and the vibrant green trees looked kind of grey/green, the brilliant blue sky looked like a grey/blue. Everything was dull. I couldn't seem to find any joy in the life surrounding me. Consciously I knew I had plenty of things to be happy about, but somehow on the inside my ANTs were out of control and were telling me that *'I was a nobody, not worthy of happiness'* that *'I couldn't achieve anything in life'* and *'Nothing in life was beautiful, not even myself.'* When did those ANTs start?

I was almost fifty when I decided to take up singing in a band again. I began singing when I was in my early twenties, and I really enjoyed it. I took to it like a duck takes to water. Even though I couldn't read music very well, I was still able to sing by ear and get quite a lovely tune out of my vocal cords. My singing teacher was quite impressed with how I could listen to a recording and then reproduce the song as long as I had the lyrics in front of me, because I had a terrible memory for words. I went on to perform in over twenty stage musicals over the years, but it took me forever to learn the script and lyrics I needed. Relating to the songs helped my musicality. If the lyrics story and music really blended well, I was able to remember them much better.

When I was down or struggling to get through anxiety attacking my self-confidence, I'd put on some music, and sing and dance around. It didn't matter where it was, whether I was in the living room, in the shower or out in a park, sometimes I would just sing to myself at work. It was funny. I often found opportunities at work to sing to my patients or my colleagues. I put sticky ECG heart monitor dots on the bottom of my shoes and did a little tap dance sometimes too. If it was someone's birthday or if something funny happened and it reminded me of a particular song, I'd just start singing it and then we'd all laugh. The laughter helped. I wasn't always able to laugh, but their laughter helped me somehow. I sang Neil Diamond's 'Sweet Caroline' to a colleague, Carolyn, on her birthday. I got the whole operating team of doctors and nurses to all join in. After all these years we still happily giggle about that day. Music creates memories, bonds that are long lasting.

While in my mid-forties, I found myself single again, looking for new friendships and more, going back on the dating scene. I frequently went out clubbing, to salsa dance nights, wherever there was music and people to meet. Often, I sucked up all my courage and I went out on my own. I would always throw a smile at someone on the dancefloor or at the bar and end up chatting as the night went on. I was often one of the oldest there, but I didn't care.

I tried anything, even using dating sites on and off, to meet new friends or prospective partners. I really began to think there was no hope. I got on dating sites in the first place because as a nurse I was working odd hours, and it made it difficult to organically connect with others. There was an inability to have regular outings or hobbies, so the chances of seeing the same person out twice was rare. Building a relationship over time was near impossible. It all seemed so rushed with me and my approach of, "Hi, I know I just met you two hours ago but If I don't ask now, I may never see you again. Can I have your number?" simply scared people off. Each time I ventured out of the house I felt as though I was on a speed date outing.

The clubbing scene was okay but then one week after my fiftieth birthday, COVID-19 Pandemic lockdowns hit and I thought, *'How on Earth am I ever going to meet someone now?'* There was nowhere to go out and meet people. Like countless others around the world, I went online again. All those dating apps out there that are supposed to find your perfect match but what is a perfect match? I wrote out what I thought I was looking for in a partner, a match that I hoped would be out there for me. There were fewer opportunities to meet people face to face and I was doing my best to remain COVID-19 free for myself, my colleagues, and my patients.

As a trauma surgical nurse, I don't work with the same teams all the time. I might come across over a thousand healthcare professionals every year. Some I work closely with every day but most I rarely see. So even at work, developing new friendships, making connections, was hard. I began to think there was no hope of finding a partner who I could truly connect with and spend time with. The rosters were making it impossible. Everyone wanted to meet on the weekend, and I worked most of those, so I told myself, *'I'm done.'* There's no sense staying on these sites and trying to find a match. *'I'll just start singing again and try and get the odd weekend gig performing in a band.'* So, I joined a band and was really enjoying learning the intricacies of a new form of music that I'd not sung before.

I got myself out there and I learnt the words, and I think I did a half-decent job. Then came the ANTs. I listened to the other performers, I saw them scheduling performances in various bands and they all looked so much more professional than me. I'd forgotten how much performance I had done in the past and how much experience I really did have. I started comparing myself to them. My thought patterns started to loop. Every mistake I made in band practice my ANT's made me feel like I was just *'starting out all over again.'* As if was my first singing lesson and I had no idea how to make the notes come out. How could I combat this? The feedback was positive from most band members and the audiences. Somehow that wasn't enough in my own head. Every note, or word I got wrong just got my ANTs telling me *'I wasn't going to be capable of singing again in any band.'*

All this did was make me feel sick to my stomach and short of breath when the nerves kicked in. I tried to deep breathe; the stress caused my brain to forget the lyrics. I didn't talk to the band about this, I'd go off to the toilet to gather myself, and then when I came back, I would carry on. The lead singer never seemed satisfied with my performance. All the while my ANTs kicked me repeatedly for having to leave mid-practice, imagining that everyone was looking at me like a failure. I got through it, though, for the few years I was in the band. We performed online and even did live performances together. During COVID-19 we did have a lowered audience capacity at times. It's only now that I'm not in the band anymore, that I look back at the recordings and realise what I had actually accomplished. I was performing again, and I could see how happy I looked when I was on stage singing and dancing to the music. I really did have fun, yet, on the inside, the ANTs were eating away at every little bit of happiness I was trying to gain for myself. When I left the band, I was miserable, I was so lost. I thought what would be my next step now, if *'I couldn't even do what I had done before?'*

All the 'would have', 'could have', 'should haves' kicked in. I was thinking, *'I should have stuck it out'* And, *'If I had have stuck it out, I could have succeeded.'* I could have stayed with the band. Maybe I could have left my evenings and weekends of nursing and started performing again, doing what I loved. *'I would have been so happy.'* I blamed myself for not having the strength to stick it out longer, changing shifts at work to make more rehearsals and gigs. For not putting in 200%. I began to wonder if anyone would ever take me on in the future, since I had left this band so easily. Well, it just wasn't the right fit for me. It wasn't the right time. I didn't have enough self-confidence to push through.

The worry ANTs that were circling, overwhelming me with emotions. Honestly, most people that watched the YouTube videos or came to see me perform live were full of admiration. It was me that didn't have that self-praise. That's what I needed to find. By ruminating and looping, my subconscious was trying to solve that problem of not feeling as though I was doing a good enough job. There was sadness that I didn't seem to be able to pick myself up from, I was focusing too much on being perfect. My subconscious was fighting to find my own self-worth.

## Discovery Time

Being perfect doesn't really solve anything. You must risk making mistakes. It's while problem solving you fix the mistake and create your path towards perfection. I say towards perfection as it is really a goal that none of us can ever achieve. You're complimented when you get full marks in a test, that's perfect. The test change tomorrow, so is your effort from yesterday going to pass tomorrow's test? The goal post has been moved. Perfect, it's only perfection for a fleeting moment. The next moment, it's gone, everything's shifted. The world keeps spinning and so does your brain. When you realise you can't be perfect, your brain loops out of control.

You ruminate in the belief that you can gain insight into solving a problem, but what you end up doing is looping around the same problem without any solution. You end up concentrating too much on how others see you. I was overfocusing on imagining how the audience, the lead singer, and the others in the band would see me. If they would think I was good enough. Focusing on all that imagined lack of worth inadvertently stopped me from putting one hundred percent into the performance, or even into the practice.

## Own It

While looping you create ongoing unresolvable stress. The only way to resolve it would be to stop then restart again with a completely different mindset. To jump out of the loop, to skip out towards a more positive way of thinking. You must somehow find ways to let go of the emotional pain that you have been holding onto. Move on from your own expectations of yourself and your intrusive ANTs.

*Thoughts are just crap in your head.*
*Just because you think it does not mean it is true.*[11]

That's where I suggest you start too, in realising that your thoughts don't make you, you. It is possible for you to control and choose what you want to think about. To put a stop to your looping, the rumination. You have a choice whether you want to dip down into the sadness of continuing to march with your ANTs on their downward spiral. Or to spray them and stamp them out, all the while being kind and gentle to yourself.

Just like wild animals, ANTs can be tamed. Have you ever watched a good animal trainer at work? They are confident, gentle, consistent, and firm in their approach. They show kindness to the animal. Rewards are given for good behavioural progress. Slow and steady gets the job done. They know there is no sense in flogging a dead horse, the horse isn't going to miraculously come back to life and work for you. Similarly, the ANTs are alerting you to a fear that must be vanquished and to do so you must challenge it gently. Question and stand up to ANTs consistently and often.

Something that my father said that stuck with me from when I was a child was,

*I'm a want to be optimist,*
*but I'm so much of a realist that I just can't be an optimist.*[12]

He told himself that so many times that he truly believed in his self-limiting ANT When I looked at my dad, I always saw him achieving things and putting his best foot forward to say 'yes' and just go out and do. I don't think he was as much of a realist as he believed in his own mind. He really was quite the optimist; he always gave things a go with the hope and belief it would work out. It is all about what we tell ourselves. It's about stomping those ANTs that get in there and say *'You can't'* when clearly you can.

## Action Time

- **Calm ANTs**

Time to start fighting back at your ANTs with the spray, the shovel, the shoe. Beat them from within and move towards peace and calm in your life. Badass Diary time!

1. **Notice** the ANTs when they come into your head.
2. **Thank** your brain for the thoughts.
3. **Be kind** to yourself and breathe.
4. It's time to **act**.
5. **Write them** down. Get them out of your head.
6. **Question it, challenge it**. Do not believe the thoughts that are there on the page in front of you. Pick them to pieces. Pick them apart.
7. **Get curious** to gain perspective about the thoughts.
   What was the problem that created the thoughts in the first place?
   Was the problem realistic or was it an imagined problem, something that you had a fear about?
   Is it reasonable or was it something that was born out of a kind of perfectionism, an ideal that you felt you had to achieve to be the perfect person?
8. **How do you feel**, physically and emotionally?
   How did you feel when the thoughts came, and how are you beginning to feel now that you're starting to pick those thoughts apart?

9. **What was the trigger** for the thoughts in the first place? Write it down, name it. Tell that trigger, "I see you, but I choose not to engage with you right now."
10. Put realistic **W.H.A.T. goals** into action to solve the problem behind the thoughts. Create them. Write them down underneath your trigger.
11. **Get proactive.** Plan the time to take the steps to solve the problem and trigger that created the thought in the first place. Find a way now to plan how to tackle that trigger.
12. **Distract yourself.** Now, here's something I don't think you thought I would say to you; distract your body and your brain. It's the only way to stop the loop. Move your body, go for a walk, clean the house, do some gardening. Sing, count to ten, anything! As long as you are physically moving and distracting yourself from the thoughts, that's exactly what you need to do right now. You've already written it down, it's not like you haven't got a plan, just distract yourself to get out of that thought pattern, that loop. Stop ruminating about it now, there is no longer a need to because you have a plan.
13. **Help is out there** if you need help gaining distraction from the thoughts, call a friend and talk it out. You've made friends now; you can do this. You can just chat about whatever it was, and once it's out there it will feel so much lighter on your shoulders, on that head of yours.
14. **Move forward** with your day.

Sometimes these ANTs will come to you at times when you don't have the ability to sit down with your Badass Diary and truly work through them. There are inconvenient times when looping and ruminating cause ANTs to come at you. You may be driving in the car or working, and you need to find a way to get back your control and concentration in the moment. That's when you:

1. **Notice** the thoughts.
2. **Thank** your brain for the thoughts.
3. **Be kind** to yourself and breathe.
4. **Breathe and distract**. Go back to those techniques that we went through in Chapter 2 and Chapter 6. The breathing techniques. Be in the moment, noticing the things around you, and then you distract your body and brain, by movement. You might not be able to get up and walk around, but you can squeeze your hands underneath the table or wiggle your ankles and toes to get the blood flowing back into your legs and feet. Just something small, any little movement to distract you from the thoughts.
5. **Breathe and smile**. You can always go back later and write it down. You know by now that ANTs repeat themselves, they come back to ruminate and loop, you can deal with each one later. For now, just survive, breathe, be in the moment and start to smile again.

## Badass Journaling

Accountability, journaling with self-kindness and transference. What does that mean? Accountability means taking stock of your own responsibility. Transference is just taking thing from one place to another. You're going to fight those looping, ruminating thoughts by going to the journaling section of your Badass Diary.

1. **Write now**, I want you to write only on the left pages of the journal. Write down how you're feeling around a chosen ANT. One of those that you were ruminating or looping on earlier. Just let it all out. Every thought you are having, every feeling you are having, get it all down on the left-hand pages of that journal.

2. **Break it**. Next, you're going to take a break. That was a lot. That was demanding work, and it may have gotten you into a bit of a funk or you might be feeling better getting it all out on a page. Either way, it's definitely time to take a break. Go have a cup of tea, a big glass of water. Walk around, kick the ball with the dog. After ten minutes or so come back for part three.
3. **Read it**. It's time to read that page as if it's not your own, but instead written by a good friend. That left page is not you anymore; it's someone else telling you their problems, their thoughts, their fears.
4. **Answer it**. On the opposing right pages, you are going to answer, solve your friends' problems. You're going to write down what you think about what they're telling you.
5. **Break time** again. It is important to get distraction and distance between each step so as not to overwhelm yourself.
6. **Accept it**. You come back to read the right-hand page response except you are now receiving these kind encouraging words from your friend.

Remember, whenever those ANTs come digging inside your brain, whenever you feel trapped by looping thoughts, counter the ANTs by giving those self-encouraging responses to yourself. If you again become fixated by past imagined failures or future '*what ifs*', you now have the tools to be positive and kind to yourself. Talk to your friends, the positive ones, and choose to be around positive people. Choose to be positive yourself. Remember, those Negative Nancy ANTs need to set off an alarm that says, '*intruder alert*' and then a response to eject that intruder from your brain.

To get you started here's my example:

- **Left side of the page:**
  I'm so stupid, why did I think I could ever sing in front of people again after all this time? I don't know what I'm doing here. I'm shaking, I feel stupid. My voice has changed and sounds terrible now.

If my friend said that to me and I knew that they had sung many times before on stage, I would be shocked to hear this level of low confidence coming from them and I'd want to boost them up.

- **Right side of the page:**
  Really, I love your voice. I think it's amazing how you can get out there and start singing again. It's a smart choice. You sound great! The fact that you haven't sung in so many years, yeah, your voice has changed, but it's an awesome change. You have such confidence in getting out there. Again, I can't believe you would think you are not worthy of a place in that band. I'm proud of you and you should be of yourself too.

This journaling is going to be your lifelong tool for beating back those ANTs every time they pop their antennae up. Every new one, every old one. It doesn't matter. Even an army of ANTs could never march over you now.

## Reward Time

This is the end of Chapter 9. Go out, sing karaoke, have a dance in the shower. Shake it all off now you have an idea of what triggers your looping, ruminating, and how to forever deal with any onslaught of ANTs.

How do you get to your core, to really know yourself and know your true values? That's up next in Chapter 10.

# Chapter 10

# Know It

Do you know what your core values are?
Do you live them or are you always a sheep, conforming to fit in?
Are you always people-pleasing at your own expense?
Can you imagine living your life without the stressful ANTs
Can you stop worrying about what others think of you?
Can you start living balanced, without stress hormones like cortisol and adrenaline spiking unfavourably?

There is a reason these two hormones get released from the adrenal gland into the body, and that's because of the internal and external stresses that come at you every day. Previously, you learnt about the fight and flight responses, as well as some hormones that can affect you during those times. These two, adrenaline and cortisol, are key in the way your body responds to stress. You learnt that adrenaline hits provide the switch to take off like a spring. Burning immense amounts of the body's sugar energy stored as glucose. Well, it's cortisol that allows the release of this glucose it to your bloodstream providing your muscles with the energy to do what adrenaline is telling them to do. Stopping your body from other vital functions, for example, digestion, growth, reproduction. Even stopping your immune system from creating the fighting cells it needs to battle disease.

When you fight ANTs, you are constantly in battle-mode, with spikes in the production of adrenaline and cortisol chronically affecting your body. As a nurse, I've attended countless lectures and discussions with colleagues about the effect of stress hormones. How stress can lead to heart disease, diabetes, and so many other ailments. Do you really want to be living like that?

Or do you want to discover your authentic self, learn your core values, and beat your anti-confidence ANTs?
To be the real you, living your life confidently and unapologetically your own way?
To attract friendships and relationships based on your true, unique self?
Or do you want to live up to the dreams of others, of society?
Regretting every day, beating yourself up, living in a land of misery and frustration? Unable to be the person that others want you to be, yet still trying to conform? Never living on your own terms, living in that sick stress?
Disrespecting both yourself and the life you have been gifted?
I think we both know the answer to those questions. That's why you are here, right?
For change!

Know It

# Story Time

Here it comes, *'I can't do anything right. I'm so stupid. Everybody says so.'* Yeah, that was one of my ANTs and I'm sure it's one of yours too. We all think this at one stage or another. Even doing something as simple as spilling a cup of coffee. Or letting go of a door as you're walking through and accidentally hitting someone else in the face, through to the massive dramas in life. My ANTs remind me even when I try to do something right, something nice for someone else, everything falls flat. I drop the ball, something inevitably goes wrong. During my mid childhood to early teens, my mum was a secretary at a gravestone manufacturer's business. My parents both worked and often didn't have a sitter for me during school holidays. I would go with her to work and just read or play games out back, but occasionally I was called to help. I was bringing in cake and tea for a client one time and I dropped a cake. Tears in my eyes, my mum looked at me and said, "Oh, you're so clumsy girl." But in my head goes my ANTs saying, *'I'm so stupid. Everyone says so.'* She didn't call me stupid, my ANTs did, I did that myself. I tried so hard to do everything others wanted exactly right, to be perfect, but it never seemed to happen.

I did everything people wanted of me. My mum wanted me to play tennis. I had no interest in sport, but I competed. I wanted to go out and sing and dance, but that wasn't what she wanted. She did let me learn the piano for a brief period, only because she was learning it herself. When she gave up, I had no choice but to give up too. It was like I was her little best friend; everything she wanted to do, she got me to do with her. She wanted to do Hobbytex, a fabric painting art that was popular back in the seventies and eighties. Then it was ceramics, pouring endless amounts of liquid plaster into moulds, sanding them smooth, painting and putting them in a kiln oven. These beautiful little finished pieces we made are on my shelf today. Yeah, it was okay. All these things filled the time, but they weren't my passion, they were my mum's.

I began to wonder what was my passion? I followed my mum from one thing to another, to another. Even though neither of us realised it, she was denying what I really wanted. I wanted to get on the stage and sing and dance. My parents kept saying to me, "Don't draw attention to yourself. If you do, you'll just get bullied more." Yeah, I was bullied by my peers relentlessly. So, when I tried to tell the kids at school that I was going to go become a famous performer, they all just laughed and said, "Who do you think you are? You can't do any of that. You're not pretty. You're just a poor black kid from the suburbs. There's no one like you on TV." At that time in Australia, they were right, and my community gave me no encouragement to change that.

So, I did what I was told, and I became a little chameleon and fit in. Just making myself what other people said I needed to be. On the inside, I was screaming to achieve my own hopes and dreams. I wanted to be treated the way I treated others. If someone came to me and said they had a dream, something to do, I helped them achieve it. I've always been like that. I didn't want to be a nay-sayer and tell them that it wasn't possible. Unfortunately, ANTs began to change the way I behaved with myself, then the way I behaved with others. When people came to me, I started throwing out, "Ah, do you really think that's possible?", "Isn't that a bit much of a risk?" Or "Do you think that's the smart thing to do?" These were my own fear ANTs and now I was throwing them out at other people, often accentuating or creating their own ANTs. I came to realise the ANTs growing in me were overflowing into others around me. Not what I wanted. That's not the kind of positive infectious person I wanted to be. I never want to be that negative Nancy again.

One day I was watching television and the CSI theme song came on. As I listened to the song's lyrics 'Who Are You' they struck me. I thought, *'I don't know. I have no idea who I am.'* I had felt so disconnected from my inner self for so long. How am I supposed to achieve anything in life if I don't actually know who I am at my core. What my core values are?

When I felt lost, I would mirror others and become a chameleon, trying to find success in the only way I could imagine. I was trying so hard to gain acceptance and love. Years on, the stress of the chameleon life was costing me my own soul happiness. I don't think anyone truly wants that. I faked it, pretending I was happy, even though deep down inside the real me was screaming, trying to get out. My core self, my dreams, that happiness I wanted so dearly. Not that long ago, someone said to me, "We used to call you smiley. What happened?" I realised I was smiley back before I lost my path. I was smiley because I was living as my true self at that stage. But then societal values at large and all my ANTs got in the way. I had lost the reason to smile because nothing was going to my soul plan. My overwhelming ANTs shrieked, 'You are not the right fit in this world, there is something wrong with you.'

I tried to model myself on other's examples. When someone popular came along wearing a particular dress, I went out and got something that looked just the same, with shoes to match. My sense of style had come from my peers and from the media. I mirrored people's behaviour too. If someone gossiped, I gossiped along with them. It was a cruel, mean way to be. I wasn't being true to myself. Afterwards I would get totally down on myself, like banging my head against a brick wall just because I couldn't break through to the kind and gentle person I wanted to be. That happy girl, smiley.

I was forever being influenced by people around me, just following their lead. Not taking the time to examine their behaviour. To realise whether it was how I wanted myself to be or not. I fell into the trap of looking to others to find myself.

> *'Always be yourself. Express yourself.*
> *Do not go out and look for a successful personality and duplicate it.'*[13]

I saw Bruce Lee say this in an interview and realised I was failing at that. I realised it was exactly what I was doing, I needed to stop it. I just didn't know how. I was being swayed constantly, and I wasn't trusting my gut instinct on who I wanted to be. I was fitting into the mould that society wanted me to be, and yet I was admiring people who were reaching out and being successful with their uniqueness. Like Bruce Lee, he was unique. I had to find my 'unique.'

He also worked extremely hard to get to who and where he wanted to be in life. He believed in himself, in what he loved, his passions. He trained others in the same mindset as himself. He performed on screen when people of his race were unable to break into the world market. He just went for it. So sometimes you do go out there and look to a successful personality, but you shouldn't go out there, as he says, to duplicate yourself in the same way. Go out there with the mindset of your own freedom of expression, your own beliefs. If you do that, you can't be stopped, you can never fail because you are being true to something deep within yourself.

Now, when I make decisions, I think first.
Is it an enthusiastic, yes?
If not, then it's a no!
Is it something that just makes me shrug my shoulders and walk the other way?
That's a no!
Is it something I want to do deep down inside?
Is it something that makes me nervous, gets a little knot in my stomach of excitement?
That excitement, that's a definite and enthusiastic yes!

When I was twenty, I realised I didn't want to have children. Everyone else told me I had to have them, because that was what you did as a woman. You were supposed to go out into the world, get married and have a family. Two and a half children, the national average at that time. It was what you needed to do for the future generation to be created, but I just didn't want them. I thought they were stressful and too much work, and I didn't have that 'mothering' instinct. I didn't hate children I just didn't want to be responsible for any.

As I grew older, I wanted to mentor people my own age, not children. Whenever I was around children, I just felt a little uncomfortable.

## Know It

They always wanted to pull at my afro hair, and, oh yes, ouch, it hurt when they grabbed it. Their fingers always got easily tangled in the fuzz. Early in school another child, who obviously hadn't seen anyone of my skin colour before, tried to see if my skin rubbed off so he could paint with it. His mother was embarrassed and apologetic. The brown didn't come off and the hair was firmly attached to my head. Being treated like this, as I often was growing up, by innocent and sometimes cruel children, left me feeling unable to imagine bringing one of my own into the world.

I enjoyed my life the way it was, childfree. Before getting married my husband and I agreed that we weren't going to have children. Years later, things changed - he became paternal. Unfortunately for us, I still didn't want children and I didn't want to settle down. I wanted to keep living life, travelling, and ticking off all my bucket list dreams. That marriage was over for a multitude of reasons, my not wanting to settle down and have a family was only one of them. So off I went off on my life path. People told me, "You are so selfish." Others would say, "Oh, I wish I had your life. You're so footloose and fancy free." "Nokids. You can live the wild life." They didn't realise living the wild life wasn't a life without loneliness. Mine hadn't been a fully happy life, no life is, but not bearing or raising children is one of my choices I do not regret. It is the choice I am at peace with. I almost got talked into having a child for a while there, but after chatting with a few friends, I realised I wasn't going to be doing that for me; I was going to be doing that for my partner. I did not want to be one of those parents who looked at their child and thought, 'I know I should love you, but you ruined the life I wanted to have.' So, I lived true to myself. Courageous and with no regrets.

I went on discovering more of my core values and beliefs. I observed those around me. Seeing what it was they did or how they behaved made me want to be like them or not. That helped reveal who I was as deep down. If someone helped someone else cross the road, or picked someone up when they fell, I thought, *'Yeah, that's what I want to do.'* So that's what I did. I came to realise I am kind, helpful, and generous, and I have so many other positive qualities too. I would look across the street and see people who looked fit and healthy, and I thought, 'I want to be strong and healthy.' I knew that my health and that of others was important to me. I set out to nurse others to health and to assist them in achieving a good fitness level. Although I didn't love sport, I found other ways to stay fit. I danced. I loved music but sometimes I danced down hallways with no music playing at all, just for a laugh.

## Discovery Time

This chapter encourages you to take the opportunity to locate and ponder your own core values. Have you ever internet searched core values? You can get sucked in deep with the varied lists and beliefs out there. Even identical twins have differing core values, beliefs, and dreams. One thing is for sure we are all individuals. In western societies, uniqueness is celebrated now more than ever. Feeling a sense of safety and acceptance of self is an important human need. So many people are wandering aimlessly, not knowing what their path in life is. It all starts with self-discovery, and that's likely another reason why you sought out my book.

Why do people seek mentors and coaches to assist them on their journey to fulfilment and success?

To be a badass!

You must dig in deep to discover your fundamental core being.

Know It

# Action Time

- **Wall of Me**

Here I have included one of my early Walls of Me.
Open your Badass Diary to build your own wall.

Observe those around you, noticing characteristics in them that inspire you.
Also remember attributes and behaviours that others have complimented you on in the past.
Who are you and what will you write on your wall of core qualities?
What virtues do you possess?
Which of your actions are you proud of?

What you are striving for, what things do you want to do in life?
Contemplate what it takes to do them, what qualities are needed to be a person who achieves those things?
What are your core values, principles, and standards for you to live by?

Add qualities and values you discover about yourself to your strong wall.
Keep adding to your wall over time and you will reveal how amazing and unique you truly are.
This wall is how you can proudly present yourself to the world.

- **Calmer Chameleon**

Changing those chameleon ANTs driven behaviours of yours is as simple as follows:

1. Stop.

2. Are you feeling comfortable with what you're about to do or say?
   Will you respect yourself after you do or say said thing?
   Does what you're about to do or say match with the core value wall that you have built yourself?
   If you can tick all three of these, then it's a resounding *yes* to doing that behaviour saying that thing.

3. If not, then it's a *no*, and it's time to reassess that behaviour, that thing that you were about to say or do.

- **Roping Off Boundaries**

It's time to start resetting your boundaries, by creating honest boundaries. Reconsider the boundaries that you've made over your lifetime of being a chameleon.

**Analyse it.** Don't stand for being bullied, pushed into being a person you don't want to be. Whenever you come across something you don't want, but that you feel you 'must' do… Stop. Take out your Badass Journal and work out the reasons why.
For example:
Are you doing it because you want to be liked?
Are you begrudgingly thinking of doing it out of kindness, because you think it will be good for someone else?
Are you doing it because you have no other choice?
Are you trying to protect yourself?
What ANTs are at play in the boxing ring here?

**Get physical.** Whatever it is you don't want to do, it's time to punch it out.
Find a comfortable space somewhere where you can move, punch out. Your own imagined boxing ring.
You're not going to connect with anything, just the air.
Imagine what you don't want to do is a punching bag dangling in front of you.
You will physically punch the imagined bag until it pops, goes poof like a cloud of dust.
**Verbalise it.** During the punching movements add create positive affirmations like,
"I don't stand for these behaviours anymore."
"I will not be manipulated."
"I will be me."
"You can't stop me."
"I choose my own path."
Add specific positive affirmations that relate to your new boundary.
Speak your affirmations out loud and proud.
Nice deep breath now, and let it go.
Watch as that cloud of punching bag dust blows away, dissipates off into the distance.
Step out of the boxing ring.
**Victorious you!**

## Reward Time

You've reached the end of Chapter 10. Go out there and do something that's a little left or right of centre. Something you love that would normally be seen as out of your square. Sing loudly. Wear a silly hat. Start a nerdy hobby. Smile at strangers, whatever tickles your fancy.

Wow, can you feel it? You're letting your soul take you to your true way of being. Be proud of your achievements so far. See you in Chapter 11.

# Chapter 11

# Respect It

Beautiful poppy in a poppy field, you grow and raise your head up above the others only to have it lopped off. That's what we Aussies call 'tall poppy syndrome'; being too big for your boots or big headed. It comes down to others being uncomfortable or jealous of your success. You showed your pride in your achievements.
Why do others want to squash your hopes and dreams?
Why can't we all just help each other?
Why do you have to shrink yourself or belittle your own achievements?
The answer is: you don't!

When you gain self-confidence, you learn to accept, encourage, and praise yourself and others. It is then that you will attract more like-minded achievers into your friendship circle. This can only breed more success. If you not, you'll continue feeling shame about your own success.

Devaluing yourself and your achievements. You'll feel unloved, dejected, rejected by everyone. You'll never really want to achieve your own hopes and dreams because what's the point if you can't enjoy them?

## Story Time

When my father would hear me bragging about something I was proud to have achieved he would go to the nearest door. There, he would pretend to cut out little curves in the doorframe so he could fit my head through. He would call me a "big head." He was proud of my achievements, but he wanted me to stop bragging about them. I'd walk in to say, "Dad, look what I got on this test," or, "Look, I won my tennis match," then straight away he'd be up and heading over to the door frame again. Encouraging me to follow him. He would say, "Okay, come over here. Let's see how big we must make that hole in the door frame this time." I began to hide my achievements. I couldn't tell him anything because I felt he didn't want to hear. Neither my mum nor my friends patted me on the back, which I so sorely needed. I was supposed to be humble. I was learning my achievements just seemed to have no value. They were a negative, rather than positive in my life, and I was becoming ashamed of success.

What was the point in trying to achieve at all? Why should I be successful if success just brought lots of criticism, shame and hurt feelings? Then it wouldn't really matter if I didn't succeed now, would it? *'Besides everyone else was more successful than me anyway, everyone else was better,'* that's what my ANTs were telling me.
Anti-success=ANTs in action.
I had to attack them. I had to stamp them out. Somehow, I was shrinking myself and my achievements so that I wouldn't stand out. So much so that no one recognised that I had been successful at anything. There were times I felt so frustrated, where I wanted to tell people of my achievements. I wanted to be special. I wanted to be seen. They were the occasions when I'd overcompensate and feign overconfidence. Only to regret it afterwards. The bold, egotistical,

show-off behaviour was not how I wanted to be remembered. So, I put my head back down and hid myself, withdrawing again. And so, my looping frustrated success ANTs were born.

I watched famous stars on television, making their living being confident, egotistical, and proud. I wanted to have that confidence somehow, but I didn't want to be mean or unkind. Later, I came to realise, it was all just for show. They had teams of people around them keeping them boosted and pumped up so that they could perform. In their downtime they are just as human as you or I. I set out to discover how to stop my own seesawing behaviours. To balance between being too humble with too proud.

Some days I was driven to compete and win against someone, anyone. On the other days I would let others win. After all, *'No one really likes a winner so what's the point of winning anyway?'* But people do like winners they just don't like winners who jump up and down throwing their success in people's faces. It was hard trying to work out how to behave, what to strive for. I just didn't know how to do that. I set out to learn about and explore different religions. My parents had put me in Sunday school at the local Baptist Church, but it wasn't really for me; there was a little bit too much fire and brimstone in it. I then started reading about Catholicism, Buddhism, Hinduism, other religions, and so many other belief systems. I have never chosen one, but I took on board numerous values, a little from each.

Then I came across karma. As I understand it, karma is simply just what you put out comes back. What others put out comes back to them too. If you were a good person and did good things, then good would come to you. Either in the here and now or in the next life, if you believe in a next life. Over time I realised that most belief systems, religions, and spiritualities seem to have some form of 'do unto others as you wish done to you,' in their core structure. So, I applied that for myself. I decided that I wanted to be treated with kindness, so I would take every opportunity to be kind. I wanted to be a generous person and that generosity was just as often returned. My behaviours were reflected. You really do get influenced by those around you. It's good to boost others up and have them boost you. We all need encouragement and praise to get through our day.

As much as I had issues with celebrating my own successes, I also had trouble accepting any form of praise. I spent my days putting my head down whenever anyone gave me a compliment. I heard the words coming out of my mouth, "Oh, thanks, but it's just….." then out would come the reason my achievement wasn't so great. The ANTs reason why what they were complimenting me on wasn't so special or important to note. Each time I saw their faces drop a little. Sometimes they would try several times to convince me that their praise was real, and I deserved their respect and admiration. By not accepting their compliments, I was actually offending them. They had put care and thought into complementing something they had judged as a wonderful thing. I was nullifying that, squashing their opinion. I decided I wasn't going to do that anymore either. There were so many ANTs and behaviours I needed to change, and the shrinking myself to be humble, avoiding being a tall poppy behaviour, that was one of them.

There are loads of songs out there that represent positivity and being proud of yourself. So many more now than there ever were before. Maybe I just didn't listen to them previously because I was so busy listening to the music on the radio station my dad would play all the time. Songs with sarcasm, striving to be egotistically perfect. Or battling the tough times and focusing on the negativity in the world. I have built myself a playlist that is all positive. Whenever I'm feeling '*low*' or '*unworthy*' and those ANTs are pushing too hard at the inside of my head. The music cracks my shell open and dances those naughty ANTs out. I have so many playlist songs now, and I suggest picking your own songs to make your happy playlist. Fill them with songs that make you feel strong, special, worthy, and capable. Ones that allow you to be proud and loving of yourself. When I need a boost, my playlist is ready to enhance my mood. Sometimes I just sit in the quiet and journal, other times I have cool cheerful tunes going on in the background, just loud enough to get me all inspired and positive.

## Discovery Time

What do you do to boost your mood from, '*why bother?*' to '*why not?*'
Do you have trouble taking a compliment with style and grace?
How do you boost your own confidence without going overboard?
Do you throw others under the proverbial bus to keep yourself on top?
Or do you fade into the distance allowing others to take all the glory?
Do you surround yourself with supportive people?

The positivity and encouragement from your friends and community builds your self-confidence. Accepting praise is essential for your growth. Allowing you to strive onward to achieve more. This in turn increases your satisfaction and happiness through your life. Compliments positively influence you and those around you too!

## Action Time

- **Compliments 101**

**Receiving. This is how you take it.**

1. **Breathe**. I know you've heard me say it before, but breathing is important. Remember, nice and deep in through the nose, and out through the mouth.
2. **Hold** a breath while imagining the compliment is true. Don't let the breath out. It prevents you answering straight away. Let the mind go towards the truth in the compliment, whether you believe it or not. Imagine, imagine, imagine. Ok breathe out.
3. **Say**, "thank you," then stop talking. No more belittling responses. No "but it was only…" or, "but it was nothing." Just say thank you and stop.
4. **Shush** your brain. Shush your mouth. You've said all you need to say.

5. **Breathe** in and out and look at the other person. See them smile. You did that for them because you let them pay you a compliment.
6. **Smile**. It can be a shy smile if you want, or a big beaming, proud smile. You're in a safe place. This person gave you the compliment, they gave it to you because they wanted to, so just let them do it. Take it with a smile.

Well done, you've taken your first compliment with style and grace.

**Giving This is how you do it.**

1. **Breathe**. Yes, you know this, you got this!
2. **Make your compliment** genuine. Say it because you mean it, you believe it to be true. Don't be wishy washy, have something specific that you want to say.
3. **Make it short** and to the point. Don't waffle on or diminish the moment.
4. **Make it spontaneous**. You don't have to spend hours thinking about what to say or how to say it. Just go ahead and say the compliment
5. **Have no ulterior motive.** Don't compliment someone to get something. Do it because it's the truth in the moment.
6. **Smile and breathe.** That's it. It's that simple. Just say it. Smile, see them smile, then smile some more. Oh, and breathe.

**Build-Up Group Game**

Healthy, supportive friendships come from watering the poppies and letting them grow in their own way. Instead of cutting each other down or teasing each other with sarcasm, try building each other up. Here are the game rules..

## Respect It

1. Everyone writes a compliment on a piece of paper.
2. Place them in a bowl.
3. This bowl can be used whenever someone needs confidence or inspiration.
4. Choose someone to start, volunteer, or do a coin toss, it makes no difference.
5. The first person thinks up a compliment (or chooses from the bowl).
6. Pay that compliment to someone in the group.
7. The receiver accepts the compliment.
8. Then the receiver pays a different person in the group a compliment.
9. The game continues until everyone has made and received a compliment.
10. Play as many rounds as you want.

A group of friends of mine play this when one of them is feeling low. They often continue until they find themselves laughing so hard that they can't go on. The compliments can be silly and funny. Just as long as they're real, positive, and true. Have fun with it, start with a couple of friends and play it as a party game. You'll end up laughing at each other, smiling, often learning more about each other than ever before as some real positive truths about each other come out.

## Reward Time

Wow, the end of Chapter 11 has come. A short chapter, but a good one full of positivity. Get out there, go smell the roses for a while because sniffing poppies could find you being arrested and thrown in jail.

Onto Chapter 12 to learn great mood control techniques.

## Chapter 12

# Control It

What is success?
How do you measure success?
Do you feel that no matter how hard you work on succeeding it's never enough?
Is it never perfect?
Do you get frustrated and angry and can't seem to control your mood?

There can be a variety of reasons for difficulties with mood regulation and control. It's no surprise that there can be another hormone at play here. Testosterone. Many people think it's just what we use to describe men's fight behaviour; we do often look at men as the aggressors in society. But women also produce and are affected by testosterone, usually at much lower levels than men. Testosterone plays a role in our moods. It can easily be seen when you look at exercise junkies, those who take testosterone shots to help them build muscle and perform at the gym. They have severe mood swings, they go from extreme happiness to extreme anger. I've seen it myself, and I'm sure many of you have too, even if you haven't taken notice of it.

I have a friend who transitioned from assigned female to male. He took testosterone shots, and with that his behaviour changed too. He started to have flushes of anger with his partner. This contributed to a temporary behaviour of emotional and physical abuse. Everything worked out when the dosage levels were adjusted, and he learnt to deal with the flushes of emotion coming over him. We don't all have experience with taking testosterone, but our bodies produce it in different levels. Depending on who you are, your gender, your genetics. Managing mood changes due to our own bodies' hormones can be difficult while you are striving towards success and happiness in life.

My definition of success is accomplishing an aim, a goal, a hope, a dream. But when striving toward success, it's often from a perspective of reaching a perfect goal. Not everything turns out as perfect as you want it to, and success might differ from your first envisioning. As perfectionists we often set impossibly ambitious standards, where nothing is ever good enough. Even when goals are achieved, we end up feeling they could still be made better. Perfectionism can be soul destroying while you traverse the road to success. Along the way mood swings of frustration and anger interfere with your journey to reach that perfect goal. If you're anything like me, you want to calm those mood swings and act with integrity, but you also don't want to take any crap.

Wouldn't it be great to free yourself of your perfectionist frustrations? To have healthier expectations of yourself and others? To change the narrative inside your own head so that you don't get frustrated in the first place. No more being seen as an angry, argumentative, hot-head with countless temper tantrums. You can improve your communication skills and resolve arguments with friends, family, and colleagues. No more losing friendships and relationships due to your moody behaviour.

# Control It

It can be easy to be forgiving when someone is temporarily very stressed, bouncing from one emotion to another. When a reason, or a catalyst can be observed as the cause of their frustrated moods, we can excuse their behaviour. Yelling, screaming, arguing one minute and down in the depths of depression the next. Still, we forgive them and feel for them, we try to soothe them; whether it be good or bad, it's these emotions that make us human. But when the behaviours seem continuous and problems can't be seen on the surface, all the lashing out is more difficult to understand. It's tougher to have any kind of empathy for that person. Well, I was that person.

## Story Time

I walked around every day just getting on with life as best I could. While inside there was a storm of emotions brewing every moment. ANTs telling me 'I wasn't worthy' and all I could think was, *'I'm such an emotional wreck. When will I ever get it together?'* I was happy when I was with someone that made me feel good. Occasionally I'd happen by an old friend or acquaintance on a street corner and practically crush them with happiness hugs. While chatting with them, they'd ask me how life was going. I didn't know how to give an understandable and restrained answer. I would cry telling them my whole family had died. My voice would raise in volume as my anger built as I explained I had just gotten divorced and lost all my current friendship group. Then the tears would well up as I explained that the only people I had stayed connected with were those who knew all this was going on in my life, the ones who were trying so hard to stop me from killing myself. I was that low. Those acquaintances would offer to take my number and call for a catch up. In reality they were so uncomfortable with my flood of varied emotions they'd disappear, avoiding all contact. I would not see most of them again.

I hadn't seen this friend for years, but I was so happy after bumping into them on a street corner. They couldn't understand why I was hugging them so tight, their connection to me wasn't that strong. I remembered spending happy times with these people in the past, but now I had just I blurted my life story out all in one hit. Understandably they struggled with a bit of conversation and then were on their merry way. I was left standing there on the side of the street thinking, *'I'll never have any friends. I'll never be able to keep anyone in my life if I can't hold it together.'* I wondered, if I kept my pain inside, to myself, then maybe I'd be able to cope, or look like I was coping on the outside. Then it would be possible for everyone to like me again.

Some friends came back into my life, while others felt awkward and ran off so as not to be forced to deal with my emotional outbursts. I'd see families happily cooking over the barbecue, eating lunch in the park and I was so jealous of them. I'd never have that again. My family's all gone. I'd tear up and think, *'It's not fair they have it so good.'* Then conflicted after realising my selfishness, my thoughts would switch to kind thoughts of, *'It's okay, let them have their happiness.'* I never wanted anyone else to know, to feel, what I was going through. I wanted everyone else to have a happy life. My ANTs said, that *'A happy life wasn't for me,' 'I was too angry and frustrated to be happy.'* Everyone had left me or died, so how could I be happy? Obviously, *'There was something wrong with me.'*

I wanted to blame my life on someone, something, anything. I blamed it on God, the universe, the guy next door, the woman at the checkout, anyone. I would get angry and frustrated and speak out of turn at them, all because my cup had runneth over. You've probably heard that analogy. Well internally my emotions stood crying in a cup, my tears filled the cup up and I kept crying. The cup filled and overflowed over the edge. I was drowning but I couldn't stop that waterfall of emotion coming from within me. On the outside I rarely ever cried, but my pain and sorrow were coming out in diverse ways. With anger, with confrontational behaviour. Like the expression- if you don't heal what hurt you, you'll bleed on people who didn't cut you.

I needed to be in control. I wanted to be right, to be considered knowledgeable. Normal conversations turned into a yelling match with people eventually asking me to calm down. My response was to yell, "I am calm." But deep inside I knew I wasn't, and they were only getting a taste of my emotion; it was much more devastating inside. I learnt to remove myself from situations that caused me to be so confrontational, like going off to the corner of the party, watching everyone else have a fun time. I knew there was no way I could jump into any of those conversations without getting loud, obnoxious, and annoying everyone around me. How was I to stop my emotional lashing out? I wanted to walk softly and carry a big stick. The stick was supposed to only be for the people that were there to harm me, not for every single person I saw in front of me. I wanted to walk softly on the earth and deal gently with others, to speak calmly. Conversations with people instead of confrontations was what I so deeply desired to get back to.

I had a good group of friends that gathered at one couples' house every week. It was a welcoming home where we were all able to pop in anytime on a Friday and have a few drinks, chill out, and end the week. The husband and I would sit at the table out the back, him with a smoke in one hand and a scotch in the other, and me with my bottle of wine or more often two bottles of wine. I drank heavily back then to block my internal pain. I only had to stumble about three hundred metres up the road to get home.

Many conversations were had over that table, and his and mine often got hot headed as our opinions would start flowing. I would argue relentlessly to defend my position, but we were both a little stubborn that way. We couldn't see each other's side of the conversation, yet we refused to agree to disagree. We would just keep going until everyone at the table had gotten uncomfortable and walked inside. That was when his wife would come out, on cue as he was slamming his hand on the table making another point, she would say, "Are you two all right out here?" Instantly we would stop, look at each other and say in unison, "Yeah, we're fine, we're just having a conversation. We're having a good time. We're best mates, aren't we?" And we would hug each other. We were just releasing our frustration, letting it all hang out. We weren't really arguing, we were just allowing each other to spout forth opinions no matter how insane they were until we felt better. Until the anger was gone, then we could just laugh and joke and carry on happily with everyone else. Everyone would filter back outside, realising that we were okay and not in the midst of murdering each other.

And there it was, our stress relief, not the healthiest communication, but it worked temporarily. This heated conversation wasn't something I could do with anyone else, but he and I trusted that in the end we would still care for each other. We would still allow each other to have their own opinion, and we would eventually agree to disagree.

I've gotten better at that now too. I don't get to that heated stage very often, but when I do there's usually a reason for it. It's not just a random burst of emotion rearing its ugly head. Now, when I start to feel that frustration and anger welling up with inside me, that testosterone burst trying to break free, I repeat phrases inside my head, like *'not my circus, not my monkeys.'* Occasionally I'd hum or sing the song from the musical Westside Story, Cool. It was a great moment in the musical where all the guys managed to calm each other down and stop each other from getting into a fight because, *'now wasn't the time.'* When I sang songs like this it worked, I calmed down. I walked away from arguments. Even the ones I wanted to start. It really wasn't worth it anymore. There was no more blame game to be had. Not after I realised, I wasn't the angry perpetrator, nor the victim in the heated argument anymore. I wasn't needing to rescue anyone from the heated situation, nor be rescued myself. The drama cycle dissolved. When I recognised this, I could put a stop to it. There was no need to continue this cycle.

## Discovery Time

Nothing in nature is perfect and darling, that includes you. There will often be times when you need to bring a song or a mantra to mind calming yourself, to take a deep breath and step away from a situation.

## Control It

There might be times when you go forward into an argument, you are never going to be flawless. Trying to be perfect every second of the day is just setting yourself up for failure. You are human, not a robot. Imperfection allows for growth, growth creates change, and change is good. Some of the best discoveries were born out of mistakes. For example, Penicillin or mould juice, discovered growing on one of microbiologist Sir Alexander Fleming's experiment culture dishes in his laboratory. Then there is Viagra which was originally created for treating angina, heart pain. There are many things born out of mistakes. There's no need to feel guilty for them; own them, use them, make amends, then move on. You are not your mistakes. You are not damaged beyond repair by them. Your scars are just part of you that shows your human discovery journey through life.

These are interesting philosophies that have come out of Japan. I discovered them when I was living and working there in 2006. Wabi-sabi, which is the art of embracing and showing value to something that is imperfect, flawed, or damaged. Secondly, Kintsugi, an art of repairing pottery, as well as a philosophy. Taking the broken pottery and repairing it with something beautiful for example, gold or silver. When that pottery is repaired using those metals it becomes something more beautiful and valuable than before it was damaged. That little gold line or crack in the piece of pottery is something special. The history of that piece of pottery was never again going to be disguised or hidden.

Mistakes are not something you need to hide, they are a part of your history. They are something to learn from, to evoke change from as well. we need to keep them around as a reminder not to repeat the same error again. If we break a cup, we are reminded how we broke it, so that we won't break another cup the same way. We repair it, reuse it, and continue to see its value. "Waste not want not," as my miser mum often said. It's amazing, really, it's such a beautiful thing to do with an object. I think it's something we need to do for ourselves, to embrace those philosophies onto our own bodies and minds. Valuing change is how you find your way to success.

## Action Time

Anger management is a serious issue and here are some methods to calm yourself, without holding on to suppressed anger.

- **Calm Emotion Moment**

1. **Observe**, listen to your own body's responses. For example: your heart rate and breathing.
2. **Calm** yourself by using the techniques that you have mastered in earlier chapters. For example: breathing slow and deep.
3. **Be present** in the moment, repeat your mantras, your songs quietly to yourself.
4. **Remove** yourself from the situation if necessary.
5. **Wait**. Only when the calm has come to you is it time for the next step.

It all sounds easier said than done, right?
But it does become easy with practice. It becomes easy peasy!

- **Accepting Emotions**

Accepting emotions when there's a safe place to do so can be calming. It is really rewarding to not let emotions fester within, growing like a volcano until they explode from you like hot red lava.

1. **Breathe** deep.
2. **Feel** the sensation or the emotion and continue to breathe through that emotion. Just let it sit there.
3. **Observe** the emotion with curiosity. Just like you're a scientist looking at a specimen in a bottle, you are the specimen in the bottle. Observe yourself.
4. **Let it be**. Simply let the sensation be there. Don't try to push it away. Make peace with it. Let it run its own course. Let it just be.

5. **Recognise** you find the feeling unpleasant, but remember it is only a feeling, you can choose how to react to it. You are okay, you are safe, choose now to accept it.
6. **Thank** your body and its protective response, thank your mind, and move forward with your day.
7. **Breathe** in and out more calmly because you now realise that the emotion is not you and you are not the emotion. As it leaves you, let it go.

That's step two done, now you have calmed and accepted your emotions.

- **Conversation Resolution**

First things first.
Are you feeling calm?
Have you accepted and released your emotions?
Yes! Finally, now is the time to express your needs and how you wish to have them met in an assertive and non-aggressive, respectful way. You can plan your resolution conversation.

1. **Organise**. Decide on a place where you would like to have the conversation, somewhere you will both feel safe. Choose a convenient time for you both.
2. **Emotional safety**. Organise a responsible person to be a silent witness/mediator if needed. Someone to sit quietly, with no input except to call a brief time out if necessary. Someone with whom you both feel safe and calm around.
3. **Consideration**. Ask the person if they wouldn't mind coming to have a chat. They will know you would like to get something off your chest. They may need to be reassured that they will have the opportunity to speak and that you are willing to hear what they have to say too. They may be anxious or curious and ask what the topic will be. Feel free to give them a brief heads up but don't go into details.

4. **Speak calmly** with a neutral tone. Don't allow yourself to race the conversation or raise your voice. If that does begin to happen just take a deep breath to slow and calm yourself down. This will help the other person hear what you want to say. After you've finished speaking, thank the person for listening and invite them to raise any concerns or discussion points.
5. **Further consideration**. It's time to listen to the other person. Remember, you need to truly listen, there might be something you hadn't considered in the whole situation that they're going to bring up. You need to be considerate in listening to them as much as they were when they listened to you.
6. **Continue** with this to and fro discussion until you both feel heard and understood.
7. **Resolution**. Now is the time to decide how you are going to resolve the issue.
Are you and the other person in agreement?
Have apologies, acceptance of apologies, been made?
Has the matter been settled?
    - If **yes**, it's time to thank the person for the conversation and move on.
    - If **no**, is it now time to agree to disagree. To move past this matter. Is it time to negotiate a new way of maintaining the relationship, or time to go your separate ways? This will depend on a situation-by-situation basis as sometimes there may be no way you can avoid contact with this person. You may need to both swallow your pride, agree to disagree, and find a way to manage a respectful way of remaining in contact. For example, work colleagues or family members are not always people you can just cut out of your life immediately or completely.

It all comes down to communication. I have set the skills out simply But when you're in the heat of a moment, often a few steps get thrown out the window. It's then the whole conversation falls apart. That's why your first step is to reach back into observing your emotions and calming yourself before entering these important conversations.

Reader, how's your Badass Diary journaling going?
Are you still completing it regularly?
It ought to habitual by now. If not, no time like the present here is your friendly reminder to continue forming your journal habit. If you have, review your journal entries. Look up the choices you made and the reasons why you made them.
Are they changing?
Are you becoming kinder to yourself?
I'm sure you are, and by now you'll be finding yourself growing kinder to others.

## Reward Time

It's for your permission to have fun. Extroverts, I want you to go out and be goofy, jump up and down in the street, go for a run, get your body and lungs moving. Introverts, go sing in the shower when no one else is around.

You're almost there. You can see those hopes and dreams and that success coming your way. See you in Chapter 13. Blow off the superstition it may be unlucky for some, but not for me or you.

## Chapter 13

# Go For It

What hopes and dreams have you reclaimed?
What ANTs have you unpacked from within your baggage, at the bottom of your case?

Now you have cleared the ANTs' space in your brain, you have the power to go out and realise your dreams. Are you wondering, *'What if I relapse into old habits?'* Well, the confidence that you've built in the last twelve chapters will keep you on track. Just bookmark your most difficult sections and go back to them when you need a reminder or some extra practice. Don't forget you have your Badass Diary to keep you travelling on the road to success too. Follow your hopes and dreams down that wondrous path.

If you don't follow the steps, you'll continue to feel hopeless, stuck. We all know you don't want to live a life of regrets. There was no way I was going to allow myself to live with disappointment when it came to my artistic pursuits. Pluck up your courage and go for it.

## Story Time

As I mentioned in Chapter 8, I wanted to act, dance and sing. I wanted to perform. I got that chance in the Eisteddfod. But that that wasn't my first performance. My first time on stage was in primary school, and it was that experience that spawned my creative bug. I was given the role purely because my teacher could see that I was struggling with bullying. The teachers created a little easter bunny play with a bullying theme, thinking it might help me and others to get the bullies to stop pushing some of us around. Weeks later, there I was up on stage as the star of the show. With my oversized colourful lollipop, pressing the button on the remote control of the robot dog to make it walk across the stage with me. The mean kid character came on stage and called me names, stole my lollipop, and kicked my dog. My character ran crying from the stage. The mean kids froze in position as the easter bunny entered and sprinkled glitter everywhere, the bunny left the stage, and my character came back out. The mean kid characters were now nice to me, they gave me back the lollipop and they petted my dog. They became my friends, onstage. The curtain came down and there was applause from all our parents in the audience. As the curtain rose, we all sang a feel-good song, something by The Beatles, I think, and the parents in the audience joined in.

I wish the world could be like that. But when the play was over, I walked off that stage and went out the back to get changed, the bullies pushed me down the stairs. The toy dog broke. The world wasn't kind, it was difficult. The bullies told me there was no way I was going to be the star of the show ever again in my life. I believed them. Although I tried so hard at everything my ANTs convinced me *'There was no way*

## Go For It

*I was ever going to succeed.*' I let those ANTs grow from such an early age. I beat those ANTs down eventually, though. Years later, at the end of high school when I was in the Rock and Roll Eisteddfod, invited to perform by a good friend, I trusted that everything would go well. She found so many of us misfits and put us all into her performance. It was such a positive experience and I loved it.

When my parents banned me from studying drama throughout high school, I knew I had to find a way to stay in touch with a drama circle. I had a high school friend, she played the flute and her brother the saxophone in the music department. They would go to see all the musical theatre shows and sometimes play in the music pit at the local community theatre. I would go along, see the shows, and hang out with them afterwards. They introduced me to the cast, and I got to go backstage to the green room and sit in the music pit. There was a bar downstairs with a piano. Everyone, cast, audience, adults, and kids, would sing show tunes or just hang out there after the show. I loved it, I never wanted to go home. I wanted to be a part of it, but again, my parents said no. I waited until I was in my mid-twenties and it was those friends who convinced me to go and audition for an amateur theatre musical chorus role. I did it! I auditioned, and I got in. *'A star was born,'* I thought.

I took vocal, dance, and acting lessons. I planned and prepared for success, and there I was, up on stage, having a blast. I continued, through my twenties and thirties, doing seventeen amateur theatre musicals. Those experiences, plus all those singing lessons, led to me singing the backing vocals in a couple of bands. I was privileged to sing at my good friend's wedding, too. That was a wonderful opportunity for me to be able to bring joy into the lives of two of my close friends by singing for their first dance. I just loved it. I couldn't believe I was there singing the Etta James, At Last, a song that I dearly loved. I wasn't even nervous because everyone's eyes were on them; I didn't take that moment away from them. The guests thought it was a recording, until they turned around and realised, I was singing the song to a backing track. Hearing this later made me laugh. I don't think I had ever had so many positive comments on my singing one song at that stage in my life.

One thing led to another after that. I sang, I danced. I auditioned for university and got into a drama class that only accepted forty students per year. I worked hard and my grades were excellent. At the time I hadn't completely silenced my ANTs. I couldn't understand how 'a stupid girl like me with no talent' was succeeding in these artistic pursuits. I had even been chosen for roles on television in commercials and a TV series, so I thought, 'Why not do a play?' I called my show Grave Letters and performed it at the Adelaide Fringe Festival. There I was with my own solo show, I decided on it and just got it done. I planned it. I achieved it. I didn't know how, but I made the decision to follow that dream from childhood.
Slowly but surely, I strove ahead, and I finally got there. Not by saying "no", not by listening to my ANTs.
By saying "yes" and working hard to achieve my dreams.
I'm sure to go on stage again, but right now I'm just loving writing. I've written poetry and had it published. Now I've written this book.

## Discovery Time

I'm attacking life with the confidence to believe that I can, and it's all because of the techniques that I've shared with you in this book. Things I do for myself every day. That's how I follow my dream as it changes from one achievement leading to the next. I don't try anymore I just do, like Yoda:

*'Do or do not. There is no try.'*[14]

Your ANTs say you are not able, not capable of achieving your goals, your dreams That you lack the confidence or the know-how.
Get rid of the ANT word 'no'. Make up your mind and choose to say "yes." You have the tools now. Keep practicing, until it's second nature. That's the way to do it all.

# Go For It

You are never going to stop learning. Everything you have discovered here will travel with you . Success is all about doing. Growth is infectious. It's about taking the calculated risks to achieve your hopes and dreams. Those little failures along the way are not anything to get hung up on, they're just little bumps in the road. They help you because remember failure is a necessary part of learning. You can choose to use your mistakes, to push forward and be badass. Keep on track, go, and get to it.

## Action Time

Your quick reminder and personal relapse prevention guide:

1. **Understand it.** Don't forget, to carry your Badass Diary for journalling. Doing a little bit of mirror work every now and then to recognise what ANTs need to be squashed.
2. **Conquer it.** Remember to breathe and say your affirmations to boost your confidence. Imagine things you love, want and need coming to you. Remember to write your dreams down. Make plans in your Badass Diary.
3. **Trust it.** It's all about performing forgiveness and trust. Find your gooey eggs.
4. **Silence it.** Load your time with quiet moments. Practice your impulse control. There is no need to fill every space with noise. Take time to connect with yourself and with others.
5. **Energise it.** Daily use of your personal body, mind, and soul plans – work-life balance, energising nutrition, easy get moving, restful sleep, and chill out. Keep motivated by continually changing your certificate of achievement displays. Achieve your goals, then write up new ones. Monitor your mood in your diary.
6. **Focus it.** Decrease your media time. Continue concentrating on your goals in your Badass Diary. Don't stop, stay in the moment with those mindfulness exercises. Five breaths and senses; see, hear, taste, smell, and feel.

7. **Face it.** Acknowledge how you feel both emotionally and physically. Work through problem solving to gather the knowledge and resources you need to get through whatever threats are in your way.
8. **Share it.** Gather your rock pool of people. Build your self-love in the mirror. Create your community and place yourself within it.
9. **Own it** calmly. Recognise and move forward with your left page vs right page Badass Diary journalling. Encouragement and positivity are key.
10. **Know it.** Build your wall and stay true to your core values. Challenge those chameleon ANTs behaviours. Reset your boundaries and punch away all the negativity and expectations placed upon you.
11. **Respect it.** Accept compliments, give compliments, and play the build-up group game with your friends when you're feeling a bit down on yourself.
12. **Control it.** No suppressing your anger. Get emotions out somehow. Accept your emotions and make those difficult conversations easy. Continue your Badass Diary journaling. Getting ANTs to the surface allows you to work out exactly what you should be dealing with, so you know how to prevent relapsing into past behaviours.

- **Vision board**

It's time now to create your personal hopes and dreams board. Visualise what you dearly want out of life. You can start small, or you can start big. Just plan it out.

No one achieves their dream within a moment of making it. It's not going to happen overnight, but it will happen if you can plan it out one little piece at a time. Very few people can eat an entire apple in one bite. Why would you imagine that you can jump into success overnight? Take little bites of the apple. Plan out small steps to get you to your dream to achieve those hopes and goals. It's all in the planning.

**Step One**, recognise what it is you want to achieve. Write it down, make a creative picture board and put it up somewhere. Whatever works so that you can see it every day, which will keep you motivated.

**Step Two**, the 80-20 Rule, with the W.H.A.T. Goals, and 10, 20, 30 rules that you learned to apply earlier that will get you where you need to go. Just do a little bit of work towards your goal and before you know it.

**Step Three**, if you keep working at it, success will come. It's your vision of success that is important to achieve, not the opinions or dreams of others. Get out there, plan it out, achieve it.

The sky is the limit, but space is infinite. I choose space!

Where to next?

You've finished the book, so, it's time to share a drink with friends to share your hopes and dreams with them.

**THE END?**

**OR**

**THE BADASS BEGINNING!**

# Go For It

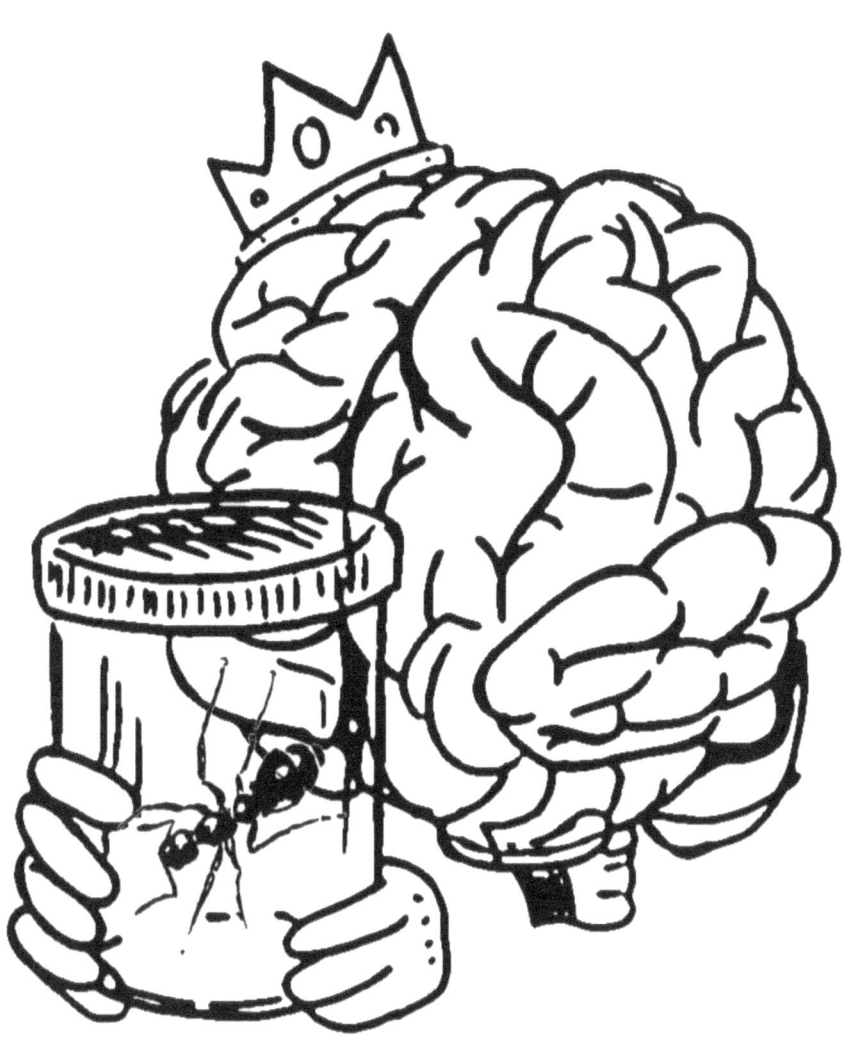

# About The Author

Donna was born in Birmingham, England to Jamaican-English biological parents. Adopted early by English & Scottish parents, and emigrating to Australia at the age of two, they lovingly raised her in the working-class town of Elizabeth, South Australia. A misfit within her community, she was bullied for her visible ethnicity, leaving her feeling intense self-hatred and struggling to find a sense of belonging. Throughout her life Donna has overcome many adversities including gender, racial and homophobic discrimination. She survived several traumatic sexual assaults and threats to her life, leading to PTSD, depression and anxiety. All that as well as her divorce, and the death of her parents, by the time she was thirty-three leaving her orphaned and without any extended family connection for the second time in her life.

Donna commenced training at nineteen years of age to be a nurse, and two years later began working as a perioperative scrub nurse. For over thirty years, Donna has continued to provide a high quality of empathetic care to her patients. While working as a nurse, she performed in seventeen amateur stage musicals. Her love of performing led her to audition for the Drama Centre Workshop at Flinders University, where she completed a Bachelor of Arts Degree in Drama and Spanish Language in 2004. She went on to write, produce, and perform in her own one woman show called 'Grave Letters' at the Adelaide Fringe Festival in 2006.

Donna spent a year living and working as an English Second Language teacher, dance instructor, and singer in Japan, and upon returning to Australia, she has continued to nurse, sing, act, and dance on TV and stage. Donna has always taken every opportunity to express herself, including having been a radio show presenter for several community radio stations. Also writing poetry, with two of her poems accepted on the PBA-FM radio well versed program and published in libraries.

Donna's inner strength always came to her aid when she needed it. The only one in her way of succeeding in achieving her goals and dreams was herself and her own negative mind. She strove to change her life by soaking up information from wherever she could and seeking out professional help along the way. Her strong passion for helping others by sharing her stories of perseverance and resilience inspired her to write this book.

Donna has touched and influenced others by encouraging and supporting them to aspire to, pursue, and succeed in living successful, badass lives. There are endless life experiences and stories bursting to get out of Donna's head not only in upcoming books but through mentoring, coaching and public speaking engagements. In answer to where to now for Donna Lavill? She states, "Wherever my passionate heart and inspired brain desires. People are my passion, so look out world, I'm coming to be a catalyst for powerful healing and badass positive change!"

# Free Downloadable Online Resources

**Yes Free!**

**Your Badass Diary!**

Your Personal Road to Recovery includes:
Lifestyle Planner Pages
Body Mind Soul Plan
Certificate of Achievements
Wall of You
Field of Dreams
Trusty Egg
THINK PR carry card
Recipes,
and more surprises…

Your journey to a happy fulfilling life started the moment you opened See You Reclaim You Be You!

Your free accompaniment materials mentioned within the book can be downloaded from:

www.donnalavill.com/badassdiary

Upon download you will also be invited to join an exclusive online group where Donna will provide you with guidance to continue developing and mastering your own *badass* life.
You will find reclaiming your inner peace and freedom super easy by being part of her online community.

For a limited time only, this secures your free subscription to Donna's online wellness newsletter,

'Reclaim the Badass You'

Within which you will find even more tricks to overcoming your ANTs. There is bonus material, like easy tasty recipes and other handy lifestyle tricks to continue living the life you deserve.

Don't forget to follow Donna Lavill on social media to stay up to date on upcoming news, events, seminars, offers and so much more. Scan for links here:

www.donnalavill.com

If you have any questions or desire further information visit the website above, or email Donna Lavill directly at the addresses below:

Email: info@donnalavill.com

# Endnotes

1. Unknown author.
2. James Baker, the former US Secretary of State.
3. SMART Goals made famous by George Doran, Arthur Miller, James Cunningham. 1981.
4. Nike.
5. Susan Jeffers, Feel the Fear and Do It Anyway, 2012, Kindle Edition, p33.
6. The five apology languages are further explained in When Sorry Isn't Enough, Gary Chapman and Jennifer Thomas. 2013.
7. Honi Ryan, Strange Embrace Exhibition, Blue Mountains Cultural Centre, NSW, Australia, May 29 - July 19, 2015.
8. Pareto Principle also known as the 80/20 Rule from the work of Vilfredo Pareto
9. Ru Paul. Drag Race, Netflix
10. Ru Paul. Drag Race, Netflix
11. Jo-Anne Hamilton, Psychologist.
12. Rodney Claude Crowther, my father.
13. Bruce Lee.
14. Yoda

# Notes

www.ingramcontent.com/pod-product-compliance
Lightning Source LLC
Chambersburg PA
CBHW030301100526
44590CB00012B/479